Running
into the arms
of
Love

Running
into the arms
of
Love

RACHEL TEJEDA MORRIS

Running into the arms of Love

Copyright © 2021 by Rachel Tejeda Morris.

Paperback ISBN: 978-1-63812-063-6
Ebook ISBN: 978-1-63812-064-3

All rights reserved. No part in this book may be produced and transmitted in any form or by any means, electronic, or mechanical, including photocopying, recording, or by any information storage and retrieval system, without permission in writing from the copyright owner.

The views expressed in this work are solely those of the author and do not necessarily reflect the views of the publisher hereby disclaims any responsibility for them.

Published by Pen Culture Solutions   06/24/2021

Pen Culture Solutions
1-888-727-7204 (USA)
1-800-950-458 (Australia)
support@penculturesolutions.com

Note to Reader:

This is a true story of a woman who grew up trying to buy love and to be accepted. She ran from her troubles. She ran from men and she ran from the Lord. The more she ran the more trouble she got into. Until she fell into a pit, this was her death bed. However the Lord delivered her; she is no longer running because she ran into the right hands, the Lord's. This story will touch your heart. This story will show you what God can do. He can turn a tragedy into a triumph. He can turn your life completely around like the fairy tales of Beauty and the Beast and Cinderella. Only this is the real life story of a woman who once was blind but she sees.

RUNNING INTO THE ARMS OF LOVE

Running into the arms of love, my symbol is a dove.
Don't shove, Oh heavenly father from above.
I will teach you how to love.
Love fails, this is not a fairy tale.
Choose to love me as I love you.
You'll know what next to do.
I will lift you up and carry you, through the hex.
Time and time again you've ran away from me; now this shouldn't be.
You would be here to stay.
I will love you anyway.
Now you finally stopped running. That's a bit stunning!
I will bless you time and time again, you are mine and you are my all.
You are my friend small or tall, be still and let me in.
So shine take my hand until the very end of time.
Still I will keep you on my mind. I am not wasting precious time.
Running into the arms of love like a dove from up above.
I am running into the arms of love.
Oh heavenly father of love from up above.
I could be his turtle dove.
In which I am made from love...

Contents

Chapter 1	Growing Up Too Fast	1
Chapter 2	Following My Dreams	13
Chapter 3	Freedom At Last	19
Chapter 4	Let It Be Me	25
Chapter 5	Get It Together	31
Chapter 6	Running From One Man To Another	35
Chapter 7	Dance, Dance, Dance	45
Chapter 8	Anticipating My First Born	53
Chapter 9	One Way Ticket To Hell	61
Chapter 10	Glimpses Of My Life	65
Chapter 11	I Stand In Awe	69
Chapter 12	Healing Takes Time	79
Chapter 13	The Reunion	89
Chapter 14	Meeting New Faces In Different Places	101
Chapter 15	What's Your Pleasure?	115
Chapter 16	Be Bold	129
Chapter 17	Right Is Right	137
Chapter 18	Answered Prayers	143
Chapter 19	When Angels Appear	149
Chapter 20	Springs Of Joy	165
Chapter 21	Inclination	173

Chapter One

GROWING UP TOO FAST

My nickname is Tiny. When I was born, I weighed only three pounds. I had to wear doll clothes. My twin sister lived only a few hours before she died. I grew up in a duplex home. This is a dysfunctional family in a dysfunctional house. My aunt and uncle lived downstairs along with their ten children. Six of us kids lived upstairs. I am the second oldest; I have one older brother, two younger brothers, and two younger sisters. Mom had lost two babies or we would be eight children. My uncle was an alcoholic. My aunt was good at winning money on her bingo nights. Many years down the road my uncle quit drinking for good. This was a positive work done in my uncle's life. It was good to see him sober for good. The time came to go back to school after summer break. My cousins all had their wardrobes ready for school, and all ten kids got to go to the state fair. I don't know how they afforded it. Money went a long way in those days.

Once there was this man who just drove up and down the street. Just looking and looking, as if he was trying to find something to do. I was a little afraid. I believe my God was looking out for me. Once in the winter my parents sent me to the store, to get a Sunday paper. The streets and sidewalks were icy. I kept falling down trying to get up the hill. I threw the paper up the hill then tried to climb up the hill. I just slid with the paper. It took me twice as long as normal to get home. The paper was torn and wet. It was a mess. I thought my dad was going to whip me for bringing home a big mess of paper, but I was surprised. He didn't. He looked at me then looked at the paper. He said come on, come inside. No matter the reason, no matter the season. Even if it was below zero raining or hot, I had to go to the store a lot. Sometimes I carried a bunch of change from the piggy bank. This was embarrassing. Sometimes mom made me go twice a day because she forgot to tell me to pick up something. Sometimes I cried all the way to the store. I don't know why mom didn't send anyone else. If I played around on the way home, my dad would be waiting. I was afraid to go into the house. I would be having fun walking home with my cousin, Toni. She loved to talk. My parents called her motor mouth. She didn't talk bad, or gossip, or swear, or complain. She just loved to talk. As soon as I walked in the door, Dad would grab me by the hair and kick me in the butt. Then began whipping me with a leather belt. My dad was strict with me. When my other two sister's were around they got away with things. My dad and mom were not so strict with them. They became mother's at an early age. They were still in school. Young kids themselves. Mom would wake us up in the morning to get ready for school. The whole time she nagged at us until we walked out the door. I would go downstairs to pick up my cousin, Mom would yell at me to not wait for my cousin.

If I were late for school. I got in trouble. But I didn't want to walk alone, so I waited for my cousin so we could walk to school together. My mom would be watching out the window. It was as though mom was waiting for me to do something wrong so she could punish me. When I got home from school, mom would be waiting.

Once I was sitting on the toilet when mom busted open the door. She had a broom in her hand. She hit me on the head and the broom broke. I didn't even know why she was mad. Mom always said that I had a hard head. She really meant that I was stubborn. Sometimes she made me kneel on a pile of rocks, facing a wall in the corner, for a good hour. Once she had me by the hair and wouldn't let me go. She kept screaming as if she lost her mind, and lost control. She was just pulling me by the hair bobbing my head back and forth back and forth, really fast. And screaming. She was taking her frustration out on me. Something happened to mom. I believe that she had a small break down. Because mom really lost it. She was out of control, almost as if she were a balloon that had to let all the air out before it popped. Mom finally let go. Then she pulled herself together. I was glad that this never happened again. At times Mom did things to me that she didn't do to the other kids. One time I asked her why she treated me that way. She said that when I looked at her with my eyes it felt as though cold water was thrown on her. She said that I was the oldest girl and she wasn't sure what to do with me. Mom says she can't remember doing these things to me. At times I felt like I didn't belong. I felt like Cinderella with two step sister's my second eledst sister was mom's favorite one. But it was my baby sister who was favored by all of us. She was spoiled by everyone. I got her a Ronald McDonald doll that teaches kids how to zipper, snap, and tie, and button. She had it most of her life. Then one day she was looking for it. She couldn't find it. She was sad. Because this was an antique.

Dad was a good provider. He was a meat butcher slaughtering pigs. He worked for a meat processing company called Amours. In fact all my uncles and some aunts worked there as well. Dad wasn't exactly a father figure. He wasn't someone you could look up to, as a role model. Yet we did respect him. Dad was home during the week. To whip or yell at us. He called us stupid in anger. One of the things dad did to us was grabbing us by the hair, pulling us by the hair or our ear. This was very annoying.

Dad usually kicked us on the butt then whipped us. On the weekends, dad would go out drinking, and sometimes he didn't come home. This was a regular thing. Mom would say that dad 'had amnesia again.' She was being sarcastic. Dad was just out drinking and doing his own thing, whatever my dad did. Mom always forgave him and let him back home. Mom did not know that this was love. She said that she didn't love my father anymore because of all the hurtful things he had done to her. Mom didn't realize that this was love that she operated in. Mom was usally home. Mom did the cooking the cleaning. She washed clothes every day to keep up with the families laundry. Mom kept busy. Mom took care of the house. There were times mom got a job to make her own money. Besides, mom liked getting out of the house for a while. Mom is the glue that holds the family together. She is a strange women. For this I am grateful that I inherit this quality from her. I used to always see mom eating some sort of candy. But she never did send me to the store to get candy. I thought mom didn't want us kids to know she had candy. Maybe she thought if we had seen it we would ask for some. Well one day my brothers sneaked some of her chocolate candy and ate it all up. Mom began asking, "Who took the chocolate candy?" It was really Ex-lax. Every one of us kids said that we didn't take it. Mom said okay, that she will find out in time who took it, because who ever took it will end up having diarrhea. So mom waited for the results. In the meantime my brothers gave some to our 2 little puppies JJ and Tuffy. The poor puppies had diarrhea.

Then all of a sudden my brothers began running to the bathroom every few minutes. What a price to pay! I don't think my brothers wanted to steal candy from my mom ever again. This was funny to watch the two brothers fight for the bathroom my brothers. Of course it wasnt funny for my brothers.

One day mom was yelling. I looked at her with sad eyes and said to her that I never asked to be born. This was a very hurtful thing to say. At the time I didn't know it. Mom took a while to forgive me for what I had said. When mom got mad at me, she would say to me, "Remember, you didn't ask to be born." This made me feel sad for what I had said. If I could take it back, I would. Mom did things to me that she didn't do to the other kids.

Mom frequently hit us kids in anger. She would hold all of her frustrations and feelings inside of her. Mom always said that she wanted us kids to have the same father. And that she would stick to her vows that she made on her wedding day. At times mom kept things from my dad, like things the kids did. She often said that dad would hurt the kids out of anger so she would wait for the right time to tell him. She just wasn't sure what time was right.

Mom showed me how to iron clothes. I thought it was fun. So mom had me iron a few things that didn't matter much, like handkerchiefs. I remember my brother was very .picky. He had to have the crease on his pants just right. If he didn't like the way I did it he would do it over. My dad had this whip that was made out of leather that he whipped us with. The younger kids got away with not getting whipped. My younger brother and sister put pillows all around themselves and covered themselves in blankets. They would scream and cry as if they were getting whipped. The youngest kids got away without getting spanked. Dad never even knew that he didn't spank the kids. Later we kids all laughed about it. I went to school with bleeding welts on my legs and on my arms. The kids used to look at me like I was some kind of freak. I felt ashamed, and embarrassed, humiliated.

In those days girls were not allowed to wear pants. When it was winter I wore pants under my dress, and when I got to school I took them off so I wouldn't get into trouble. There was this girl named Patsy. She liked my clothes, and I liked hers. When we got to school, we would switch clothes. And at the end of the day we would switch back to our own clothes. There was another girl that I became friends with named Sharon. She was one of the girls in my class. She loved horses, so much she read lots of books about them. I tried being like her. I also read books about horses. It turns out this was not too appealing for me. I like horses, but not enough to read all the books that exist about horses. I had to be my own self. Yet I wasn't sure what I liked and what my interests were. I didn't even know if I had a favorite color. That's about the time I flunked second grade. I believe that I played around too much. If I had homework I never took it home.

All through grade school and high school I played around. In sixth grade the teacher said if I could behave myself for twenty minutes, I could be a school patrol girl. So I said okay. I got to be a school patrol girl. It was fun.

Sometimes, when my mom or dad put their arm up to point or just move their hands, I would flinch thinking they were going to slap me. If I got a whipping before bed, my butt was nice and warm. I still sucked my thumb. I think it was some sort of security and comfort to me. I had to quit when I got my first paying job. Although I did know some grown folks still suck their thumb, I didn't want to any more. Besides I was growing up very fast. My brothers teased me. Calling me bowling ball butt. Because my butt was round, like a ball. When I walked I looked sexy. I guess thats why I got harass by men.

Mom used to tell me things that happened to me when I was younger. For instance, when I was a baby crawling on the floor, my brother stomped on my hands. When mom was potty training me she would make me sit on the toilet 3 hours at a time. She said that she spanked my butt until it was black and blue. She would tell me about other things she did to me and laugh about it. This made me sad. I thought this was rude.

I was excited to get a real job. I already did do work around grandma's house, and in her yard. She paid me. She was teaching me about saving money. In those days you could take an envelope to school from the bank. And the school took it to the bank for you. Sometimes mom sent me to grandma's to get money that I had there. Grandma lived next door to us. Grandma and grandpa owned both houses. The rent we paid was cheap, only a hundred dollars. I gave mom and dad money every pay day. They never asked me for money. I just gave it to them. I wanted to help with things around the house. Besides, mom was nice to me when i did things for her. When we had summer vacation from school, I was going to do strawberry picking. This was my first real job. I was excited. I ended up so sun burned that my back was peeling. This is the first and last time this happened. I didn't know that a minority could burn so bad as to peel. This was odd to me. Because I usually get dark in the summer.

In seventh grade, I was given a chance to make up my credits so that I could go into the grade I was supposed to be in. I ended up going to summer school and got all my credits. I jumped from seventh grade to ninth grade. Then i was in the same grade as my brother.

Dad would never let me stay over at my friend's house. I felt left out. Other kids were able to have sleepovers. Everyone was doing it. One day, dad finally said yes. I could sleep over at my friend's house. I got home sick and I wished I could go home. Dad would have yelled, and said I told you so. My friend did not want me to leave. So I stayed, so that I wouldn't make my friend sad and my dad mad. That was the first and last time I slept over at any friend's house.

Once my cousins shop lifted, and I was with them. I didn't take anything. I wanted to know what my cousins did. I got into trouble because they showed me what they had. I wanted something pretty like they got. We were at a Woolworth's department store in downtown Saint Paul. I wanted to copy my cousins. I didn't get a chance. But I got into trouble just because I was with them. My mom and dad came down to pick us up. They talked to the police. The police just gave us a warning since it was our first time getting into trouble. Just seeing the police scared us enough to teach us a lesson. We never thought about it ever again.

Another day we girls were sitting at the bus stop. We were just hanging out at the bus stop. Along came some young guys in a car. They threw eggs at us! We walked up the hill home. We were walking funny, because we were full of eggs. The other kids were laughing at us. We didn't know if we should cry, or laugh.

In grade school we all went to Riverview School. My aunt and uncle that had the ten kids lived in a house across the street from the school. One day my brother heard a bird in the brick wall of the school. He tried to help the bird. My brother put his arm and hand in the wall, then he was stuck. He could not get his arm out. The police stopped by to lend a hand. They had to use a crow bar to get his arm out. My brother was on the front page of the newspaper the next day. Everyone laughed. My mom was embarrassed, yet she laughed about it.

Once my cousins, the boys, decided to play with matches. The house caught on fire. Everyone got out the house safely. But the house burnt down nothing left of their home. Everyone was thankful that nobody was hurt. The Red Cross helped, and they put the pieces of their life back together. I believe none of the boys played with matches ever again.

Many years went by. My uncle and aunt were in the car on their way to Wisconsin Dells. Some young kids were not paying attention to their driving. They hit my aunt and uncle. My uncle was not hurt badly, he had a few minor scratches. But my aunt was in critical condition. They never did make it to their event. Every day my uncle went to see my aunt. There was progress, every day. She got out of danger, then she got to go home. This tragedy seemed to move my aunt closer to the Lord. In time she was completely healed.

Later in life this same aunt went into a deep depression. She lost a lot of weight, and gave up hope and faith to live. Her organs were shutting down. She said that she could see her loved ones that had passed away. She said that the lord was calling her home. I got a word of wisdom and knowledge. I told my mom that it wasn't her time yet. Mom was silent. My aunt started to get better. I asked my mom if she thought I was crazy when I said it wasn't my aunt's time yet. She said no, because she believed in miracles. I just prayed for my aunt's recovery. I did not feel I should go see her in the nursing home, I felt the Lord wanted me to pray for her at home. So I did what I felt the Lord wanted me to do. I knew that I didn't have to be there in person to pray for her. I knew that God could hear my prayers no matter where I was. I knew, the Lord would answer our prayers day or night. I knew that the Lord is faithful in everything. Every weekend dad would send us kids to the movies. I thought dad was being nice. He just wanted us kids out of the house. My dad usually had a hangover on the weekends. Back then things were cheap. We saw two movies. We could see the movies all day if we wanted to. I got a big box of popcorn, a giant pop, and two chocolate Kit Kat candy bars. If we liked the second movie better we had to wait until the first movie was over before we could see the second movie again, because they played both movies one after another all day long. Sometimes we stayed all day at the movies. If we wanted to watch them over and over we could. Not like today. Things were a lot different back then. Also, a lot cheaper. Money went a long ways. I had gotten my menstration while I was in grade school. I had turned into a woman. I also got my second job, a summer job. I was working with some catholic nuns running a summer school. In time, this turned into an all year round school for troubled kids. The kids were given a second chance to get their high school diploma or GED. I loved to paint and draw. So at age eleven I was an art teacher assistant working with Sister Louise. She was great at drawing and painting. She could paint a picture of people,

and it would look just like the photo. She was very gifted. I used to draw cartoons. At this time I was making a big drawing, of a picture board. Before I finished it, somebody stole it. I felt so disappointed. So I began another painting of a clown doing a trick with a dog. First I drew it, then I painted it. The nuns took this painting to some county fair, and I won second prize: a blue ribbon. I didn't even know that it was taken to a fair. What a surprise! A pretty blue ribbon. My grade school, years were hard for me and yet sometimes fun. As I grew into a teenager I battled with guys trying to have sex with me. Everywhere I went I was getting sexually harassed. Guys would not leave me alone. I was planning on staying a virgin until my wedding night. I had the old fashioned way of thinking, that I would wait until I got married. Then I would give myself to the man that I would marry. The next door neighbor friend was going to teach me how to play tennis. Well this man did not have tennis on his mind. He was getting fresh with me. I had to stop playing tennis with him. So I never did get to properly learn how to play the game of tennis. So much for that sport. I was mad again. Like grandma always said, I had a mad face. Now I understood why I had a mad face.

Grandma went to two churches. Our family was Catholic. Grandma went to Saint Matthews and Our Lady of Guadalupe. She would go to one one weekend, then the other the next weekend. Mom and dad didn't go to church. Sometimes grandma stopped on her way to church. And she wanted to know if any of us kids wanted to go. Most of the time we said no, because we wanted to sleep in.

Grandpa drove grandma to church and anywhere else she needed to go. Grandma did not drive. Grandpa was hard of hearing. So grandma would yell at him. My brother and I would laugh at grandma yelling at grandpa. Then grandpa got his license taken away. He started to feel down because he could not drive. Then the Lord took him. Grandma lived longer. Then the Lord took her as well. I do remember going to church with grandma. I remember sometimes being embarrassed because I smelled like a dill pickle. Around the holidays I would help mom cut up onions and pickles before going to church. Mom and dad went to church on the holidays. Then they stopped going at all. Us kids did not go on a regular basics.

All though, we were all baptized when we were babies. And we did make our first Communion. And confirmation. Because this is what we grew up knowing what we should do. I remember guff yin around. When I was suppose to be in class. I was outside in the winter ridding on a snow mobile. I was having fun. When I did make it to class, the teacher kicked me in he butt. He was hard and strict. Again I played around. I managed to make it through, again. I made my first commuion and conformation. Again I think they were just giving it to me. So I went through the process of being a Catholic. In the Catholic church people pray to the virgin Mary and to some of the saints. I didn't know why. I alway's prayed to God. I knew that God was the main one to talk to. I wanted to be close to him. But I didn't know how. I only knew that when I talked to God he made me happy. I really didn't know why I played around. why I was not serious when I should have been. I must of thought that life was a big joke.

GROWING UP TOO FAST

Come to me when you are alone.
Come to me all day long
I will be with you all the time.
When the sun goes down it's time to rest.
Even the birds rest in their nests.
Haven't you heard they have been blessed?

They know when it's time to rise and shine.
Don't be afraid you won't be left behind.
So take your time. Let the glory of the Lord shine.
It's about that time.
I'll tell you a story, don't be in such a hurry to grow up fast.
Take a chance and make it last. You'll have a blast.

Rest my precious one rest at last.
Don't be in such a hurry to grow up fast.
I hear you when you call.
You just have to be a doll.

Don't be in such a hurry.
Relax and give God the glory.
You are my precious one, so rest, my little one, rest.
At last.
Rest, Rest, Rest.

Some of us kids would get together and hang out together. Sometimes we played in our yard. Sometimes we played at the neighbors. Most of the time we played at our neighbor, Binge's, house. Binge lived across the street from us. Binge had a real big yard. All us kids, would play kick the can and other outdoor games there. At one time Binge had a crush on me. And I had a crush on him. Sometimes we hung out at the recreation center. They had playgrounds, and recreation center. We could play basket ball, ping pong, board games. Or just guff off. We lived in between both, so we could go to either one. One was called Belvedere, the other was called The Neighborhood House. The Neighborhood House was down by the ghetto neighborhood where low income people lived. This was the lower west side. Belvedere was all right. This is where I first saw kids drinking and getting drunk. I didn't want to try it, so I just watched them. Then I wanted to go home. In elementary school I had a few different boyfriends. One time I had a boyfriend, and his sister was my brother's girlfriend. So brother and sister had a brother and sister, as girlfriend and boyfriend.

One day I was playing house with a female neighbor. She was older than me. She was playing the husband and I was the wife. She began kissing me, like grown folks do to each other. This was not pretending anymore. After that I never wanted to play with her again. Then one day someone I knew tried to have sex with me. I cried that they were hurting me. After that they left me alone. Next a cousin tried to have sex with me. I didn't understand why I kept experenceing, these awkward, strange, circumstances. I have a mad face at times. Grandma always asked me why I look mad. Maybe I was mad because of the way guys treated me. Like I was some kind of sex symbol everywhere I went. I was harassed. I got it from school mates, the neighbor guys, acquaintances, relatives, and coworkers. Mom was usually home. When my parents were gone, us kids would look at my dad's Playboy magazines. Mom and dad used to go to the Mexican dances. We older kids babysat. I would make the kids laugh. I would put a mop on my head and pretend I was an old lady with the mop being my gray wig. I used a broom for my cane. The kids loved it. We had fun laughing. We older kids were babysitting one night when my youngest sister went into a convulsion. She had a very high fever. She looked like she was dead. We were all scared. We had to call an ambulance. They rushed my sister to the hospital. Somehow they got the fever down and my sister snapped out of danger. The whole family was freaked out. This happened one more time, then never happdned again. I got a part time job working for some people I knew who owned their own restaurant. One of the bosses kept harassing me to go out with him. His definition of 'going out' was not really a date. He wanted to get into my pants. He was married to someone I knew. I told him to leave me alone. So when the restaurant grew bigger they moved to a new location. I got cut in work hours. I knew it wasn't because I didn't do my job well. I knew it was because I wouldn't give in sexually to my boss. I was forced to quit. I began to feel very suicidal. Then again, I can't ever remember not being suicidal. I kept myself very busy. So I wouldn't remember the shame, and pain, that man has caused me. I knew there was a God. I knew He was real. I wanted to be close to Him, but I didn't know how. I always talked to God, as if He were a real person. When I talked to God, He made me happy. So I thought if I would become a nun I would be close to the Lord. Nuns were the only people I knew that were close to God. So I told my parents that I was going to be a nun. They were happy for me and proud of my decision.

When I had a day off work I took the day off of school. I would rest, I would lie down and listen to music. I also liked to daydream that I was married to a singer or that I was a singer, singing to the music that was playing. I actually daydreamed so well, that you would think that I was watching soap operas, on television. I would cry real tears. It felt good to dream. At least I was safe in my dreams.

Chapter Two

FOLLOWING MY DREAMS

My senior year in high school I went to school for two hours out of the normal school day. Then I went to work. The teacher got me a job working at a Catholic nursing home as a nurse's assistant. Back then you didn't have to go to school for the profession. You just got trained in to do the job. I was working with Catholic nuns again.

I became a workaholic, working two jobs and going to school. I began to think about going to school to become a nurse. At the time, my self-esteem and confidence in myself was very low. I felt like a failure before I ever gave things a chance, because I had been called stupid my whole life. I believed that I wasn't smart enough to go to college to get a degree. We kids used to call each other stupid for fun, and my parents called us stupid in anger. This word was used a lot in our house. We didn't think anything of it. This is what we grew up with, it was normal to us. We didn't understand that it was really harmful.

Every pay day I would take mom out to eat. Then I would spoil my baby sister. I gave money to my mom because I wanted her to be nice to me. So I would take mom out to eat and buy her things she wanted. This made mom happy, and if mom was happy then she was nice to me. This is what I wanted all the time. Of course this is not being realistic. It was as though

I was trying to buy my mom and dad's love. This is when I fell into the trap of trying to buy love.

At age eleven I began smoking cigarettes. I thought my dad was going to yell at me. He said if I can support my habit okay. My dad was a smoker also. I really was surprised. At the time smoking was cheap. I remember a pack of cigarettes cost 10 cents. Then, a quarter. Then 50 cents. The price kept going up. We could buy them from a vending machine.

I often went to Mexican dances. I loved to dance. Sometimes dad said I couldn't go, and I would cry. I had my heart set on going.

Every time I went I would meet somebody different.

Later I got a job working at the Saint Paul hotel. My cousin Toni worked with me. We worked in the coffee shop even though I wasn't old enough to work there. I lied about my age. When conventions came to town, we worked double shifts, sixteen to eighteen hours a day. This was very intense and nerve racking, but I thrived off the pressure. I loved the pressure. I thought it was great. Some other employees walked off the job. Everyone handled the stress and pressure differently. It was just crazy. We took turns to lie down and rest or take a nap. It felt like we lived there. Some of the employees did drugs. One day I was goofing off, and decided to hang on the milk machine, and the whole machine fell over. I was surprised because I was barely a hundred pounds. They fired me for one hour. Then they rehired me because I was good in my job.

Throughout the years I have gained weight and lost weight. I was usually small and petite.

My cousin's customers used to get me mixed up with her. My customers would get her mixed up with me. They called us the bobbsey twins. Our pockets on our aprons were full of money. I never needed to cash my check right away, because we had a lot of cash tips fom customers. I continued to give mom and dad money. I thought it was fun to do. They never asked me for the money. I just offered to do it.

At work people would walk off the job. Different employees have constantly come and gone.

One time a few of us employees got together across the street at a local bar to have a drink. It wasn't my usual thing. I had a friend named Ricky. He was teaching me how to drive a stick shift car, which I never got the hang of. Ricky decided to go in the Marines. He asked me if I would wait for him. I said yes, I did not know he meant marriage. Ricky and I were just friends. Never once had we ever held hands or kissed. We were only friends, strictly friends. I gave Ricky a huge and heavy necklace that looked like an oversized silver dollar that had a carving on it of Jesus. It had been made in prison. I don't know how I got a hold of it. It was beautiful. Ricky had a brother named Peter. I had a friend from high school named Judy. She and I hung out together at times. Judy lived a few houses away from me. At times Judy went to Mexican dances with me. Judy was Caucasian. I had a couple of other friends that liked to Mexican dance. Sometimes Judy and I hung out with Ricky and his brother Peter. I really didn't want Ricky to go away. Ricky said that I could rent his apartment while he was gone. I was afraid to live there alone because I did not know this area at all, plus I didn't drive. So I said no thanks. I wanted to live where I could recognize the streets, where everything looked familiar.

I did go on a date with some guy that I worked with. I don't think my dad wanted me to date this man. I don't think my dad wanted me to date anyone. The few men I have dated were ok. For some reason when I liked a guy, they would like me. Then I wouldn't like them anymore. It's like when I got the guy, I didn't have a desire to be with them. I lost interest. This happened to all the guys that I had a crush on.

I became infatuated with a man named Gene. He was half Mexican and half African American. He was married to my cousin for a couple of months. Then she got an annulment. My cousin got an annulment because family kept sticking their nose in my cousin's personal business. They believed lies, and rumors, that were spread of Gene.

Gene sang in a band. He could also speak Spanish well. He was ten years older than me. We began to see each other romantically.

One night at a dance Gene took me into a van. We kissed and became more passionate with each other as the moments passed. We became more desirable to each other. Gene began taking my pants off. This is one time I felt I didn't have to fight to keep my purity. I let my guard down and relaxed. Gene tried putting himself in me, but he was having a hard time. He said, "You're a virgin!" I smiled. I was glad that Gene was the first.

We talked about getting a Winnebago and traveling out east. We talked about Californa all the time, and getting married. I was simply following my dreams.

I BELIEVE IN DREAMS

I believe in dreams.
I believe dreams can come true.
I believe in you.
I believe you can have bad dreams.
That can make you sad.
I believe that dreams can make you mad.
I believe in dreams that can make you glad.
This is only a fad.
I believe in dreams you may have had.
I believe in dreams it's not all so bad.
Don't make a scene.
Don't yell or scream, we are on the same team.
I believe in dreams.
I believe dreams can come true.
Don't sit around looking blue.
Think of what you are to do.
I believe in dreams, dreams can come true.
I believe dreams can come true.
For me and for you. What are we to do?
I believe in dreams how about you?

I had a female friend by the name of Diane. She worked with me at the nursing home. We used to get high on marijuana together. We always had fun together. Diane thought I was beautiful, and I thought she was beautiful. She was Caucasian. One night we both went out and were up all night partying. Then we went straight to work in the morning. In the summer Diane would get a nice olive color tan. Diane and I hung out together when we didn't have to work. Sometimes she came over to my parent's house. We would get high and giggle. And laugh. Then we would get the munchies. Beginning to snack I would look around the room as if I never saw it before. Then we would burst out laughing.

I asked my brother if he could give Diane a ride home. I didn't know that he had had a drink or two. We were on Smith Street bridge. My brother lost control of the vehicle. I panicked and grabbed the wheel, and turned it to the right. There was a gas station on the left. I didn't want to crash into a gas pump, and get blown up. There was this woman watering her lawn. She saw us coming, she screamed and threw the water hose in the air we crashed into her brick wall. Somebody called the police and ambulance. I got a big bump on my forehead from hitting the dash board. I blacked out for a moment or so. Everyone asked if I was okay. I said yes. We were taken to the hospital. Mom and dad came to the hospital. They said it was my fault. If I hadn't asked my older brother to take my friend home, everything would have been all right. My dad's car was totaled. Mom and dad didn't ask if any one of us were okay. I was afraid to get into any car again for a long time.

It was getting closer to graduating day. Gene and I talked about moving to California after I graduated. That was our plan. Diane wanted to go with us. She asked her parents, and they said yes. I couldn't believe they let her go without any problem.

In 1976 Valley fair opened up, it was huge. Gene took me. We had a good time. When my parents found out I was dating Gene, they disapproved. They tried telling me that Gene was no good, and not to go out with him anymore. But Gene was my first love. I became a nervous wreck. I couldn't sleep at night. I stayed up thinking of Gene. I would write poetry. Gene and I continued to talk about California all the time, about how it was going to be. Gene said we needed to get a decent car to drive to California. So he looked in the paper. Diane, Gene, and I all pitched in together for a car. We got a good deal. We got a decent car for a good price. It was an LT D four door and it ran smooth. Everything was going according to schedule, but I remained a nervous wreck. My insides were jumping all over. It had been so long since I had felt normal or calm. Then the day finally came that Diane, Gene and I were waiting for.

We had a big night planned with a live band playing. Other classmates had parties as well, but I felt special because we had a live band. I couldn't wait until this night was over with. Everything was going according to plan. We all got our diplomas. We all were glad we had made it. Yeah, no more school! I had two cousins and a brother graduate along with me. We all went to the same school. It felt good to accomplish getting a diploma. At the same time, it also felt like it was just given to me, like I didn't earn it. I was on this program called Job Seeking Skills, where I went to school for two hours a day before I went to work.

Our class was going to Hawaii. I had the money to go. But I decided to spend the money on Christmas gifts for everyone instead. I do hope I get another chance to go there, I would like to. Our party had a great turn out. It was great. I danced my heart out. I love to dance. Other classmates were also having parties. They had records playing. I could hardly wait until the next day. I don't think I slept. It didn't feel like it anyway. I packed a few things. I wanted to write a note for my family so they would not worry, even though I knew I was crushing their hearts for rebelling against their words and doing the opposite of what they wanted me to do. With my eyes full of tears I could hardly see what I was writing. The next day I pretended to go to work. In reality I was leaving to California. At last we were really on our way to chase a dream that we had dreamed of.

I felt like a wild animal, being let out of the cage. For once I felt free. We had to go pick up Diane. Then we would be on our way. [took out senior picture]

Chapter Three

FREEDOM AT LAST

Now we were on our way to pick up Diane. Diane brought quite a few things, including a lot of stuffed animals. She put some stuffed animals in the back window, and Gene could not see out the back window. She brought her television, and her stereo. Diane brought everything but the kitchen sink! Gene and I just took a few items of clothes that's about it. In time Diane confessed to me that she told her parents I was eighteen. In reality I wouldn't turn eighteen for a couple of months. So here we are traveling to the east coast.

Gene had said he was a jack of all trades. He taught me briefly about car mechanics.

Diane and Gene did not get along. In fact they clashed big time. I had no idea that they would clash. I didn't know what to do. I was caught in the middle. I couldn't take sides.

As we kept traveling, we began to get more and more excited. As we traveled through Colorado, we thought that it was so beautiful. All the mountains were colorful. I said to Diane and Gene, "Oh wow, now we know why they call it Colorado. For its beautiful colors." We went higher up the mountains, and it got a little chillier. We saw snow at the top of the mountain. Diane and I were just wearing bathing suits. California's seventies and Minnesota's seventies were completely different.

California was a big change. I had long hair. I decided to get it cut short. It felt better short. Gene never said a word. I became severely sick from the change of weather climate. I was a big baby, scared to throw up. So Gene held onto me to assure me that I didn't need to be afraid to vomit. I was glad my hair was short, and not in a ponytail. It was warm most of the time.

We managed to get into some dumpy apartments in a horrible neighborhood. We didn't know that it was a terrible place to live.

The police and ambulance were there a lot. There were cockroaches bigger than I've ever seen in my life. Diane would scream and cry because of the roaches. Gene would tell her to shut up and quit being a baby. Gene and Diane got on each other's nerves. The Hell's Angels came, and acted like they owned the place. They would deal drugs, rape women, and beat guys up. They did whatever they wanted to do. They terrorized our apartment complex. Diane and I hid under the bed until the coast was clear.

We all got jobs. We wanted to find a nicer apartment in a better area. This was going to take a little time. We met a man that lived next door to us. His name was Jack. He had some issues from being in the Vietnam War. He would have flashbacks and crazy outbursts. We eventually brushed Diane off and she ended up living with Jack. Gene and I decided to move elsewhere. So after Diane moved in with Jack, Gene and I moved to a small town called Purupp. In the town of Purupp, we got a trailer home, which was nice. In the kitchen window you could look outside and see the beautiful mountains. It didn't look real, it looked like a beautiful painting. Gene got work, and I got a job as a waitress. At the time Las Vegas, Nevada was the nearest town to go and get groceries. Gene got a job fixing cars up to look new again to be sold. Some days Gene was to tired to go to work. I would rub his arms and hands and I would say you can do it. This would encourage him and motivate him to go to work.

One day Gene and I went sightseeing. We both came to a small town called "Death Valley". The car stopped, I was scared. We had heard of people in the past that had been stranded there and had died. But we somehow got the car going. In no time we were out of there.

I felt lonesome inside. I missed Minnesota. I had to keep myself busy. This seemed to be a pattern in my life. I also became depressed. I wanted to die. I thought of stabbing myself. I remained suicidal. I felt sad that Diane would get letters and money and support from her parents. I didn't have that with my family. I wished I could have left on good terms, like Diane did. I did miss my family. There was nothing I could do, to make things right again. I remained depressed and homesick. I felt lonesome when Gene was at work and I had a day off. It was very hard for me to be alone.

Back home in Minnesota, when the song that Roberta Flack sang, Killing Me Softly, would come on the radio, my mom would cry and think of me. I was killing her softly. Later she told me so.

I continued to write poetry. I would send some poetry to my sister. My sister thought the poetry was beautiful. I kept mailing poems to her. But I never told her or anyone how I really was feeling. When you are depressed, lonely, suicidal, and homesick, it's not a good mixture to have at the same time. This was dangerous mentally, emotionally, spiritually, and physically - if you are doing drugs. Drugs only made things worse.

I did write my parents once. I asked them if they could send a ring of mine so that Gene and I could get married. They refused.

Gene and I got a dog. He was beautiful and very smart. He was half German shepherd, and half wolf. I wanted to have a baby, so the dog was my baby. We named him Santana. He had beautiful markings. When he was hungry I told him to go get his bowl, and he would.

Gene was in the war. He was wounded. This did something to Gene. Gene could not produce children. Santana helped me not to be lonesome. I missed my friend Diane. I felt sad when I realized what I had done. I had left her with some stranger that we didn't even know. Diane was a virgin. Jack changed that, no thanks to Gene and me. I realized I had betrayed her only when it was too late. I felt sad and kept thinking I would never see my family again. Or maybe I would never see my friend Diane again. I wondered if I would ever get over being home sick.

Gene and I decided to get married in Los Vegas. I really wasn't old enough without my parent's permission, but who cared? Nobody even asked to see an ID. We came before the preacher beginning to say our vows, and suddenly something inside of me couldn't go through with it. Maybe it was the thought I couldn't see my family anymore, Or maybe it was the fact that Gene could not have children, or maybe a combination of all the above. At the last minute I said no I can't go through with this. Gene was sweet, and patient, with me. We never got into a disagreement. We never once got mad at each other. It seemed too good to be true. We had never argued or fought. We got along great.

Gene and I met this couple that lived next door to us in the trailer park. The couple came to our place to watch football. The woman had long hair. She reminded me of when my hair was long. While Gene and I were in Los Vegas, we gambled a little. I didn't care for gambling. That was not my thing. We did have dinner and live entertainment which I enjoyed very much. Bobby Gentree was singing. She put on a lovely, show.

I began to notice that Vegas had a side of town that reminded me of Minneapolis back home in Minnesota. But it sure was different to have winters without cold or snow. Maybe that was part the reason I was home sick. I missed a white winter in Minnesota. In California it was rainy in winter, just a little cool.

Nearby there was a place that people went to for healing. Some kind of anointed water, or spring brook which you could go into. People came from all over the world to go in this water that heals.

Gene took me to the beach in California. It was the first time I had been to a real beach.

I'd only ever seen a beach on the television or in the movies. The water was a beautiful color. The water burned your eyes and the waves looked monstrous. This was a real beach, not like in Minnesota. There we call rivers and lakes 'the beach.' Seeing the real ocean was so beautiful. It was just like I'd seen on television. I went down into the water.

As the waves kept coming I couldn't get out of the waves. Another wave came on top of the next wave. My heart was racing so fast I thought I would never get out of the ocean. I screamed for help. Gene yelled for me. He called out to me. He could hear me, yet he couldn't find me. The waves kept coming one right after another. I could hear Gene yelling for me. He yelled "Prieta!" This is a special name that only Gene called me. It means Dark in English. Gene called me that because I would get real dark in the summer.

At last, Gene found me. He pulled me from under one of the waves. Thank God Gene rescued me. He really saved my life. I could have drowned. We both could have drowned. The waves were so powerful. We both were shaken up. It took a while to calm down. I never wanted to go swimming again.

After this I became more and more depressed and homesick. I missed my family. I missed seeing the same old routine of things. I missed the familiar streets of Minnesota. I had no idea where my place was here in California. One day I tried to take the bus somewhere, and somehow I ended up in Hollywood. I have no idea how I got back home.

I had a thought to do something I have never done before. I decided to break into the neighbor's trailer. I was bored. They didn't have much of value to take. So I took two large speakers and two rings made of Black Hills gold. I told Gene what I had done. He never got mad or said anything to me. He just said, "We are going to have to leave." Soon people began asking questions about the robbery. Gene said if they ask where we were at a certain time, to say we were at the hospital. To use the alibi that I had a miscarriage. We knew we had to leave. But we couldn't take Santana, my dog. I cried. I did not want to leave my dog.

FREEDOM AT LAST

Free at last life is not always a blast.
So get busy finish your task.
Make every moment last.
Soon it will become the past.
So take a seat and relax.
Now you have freedom at last.
There will not be confusion and it will last.
It will be dissolution to your solution that will last.
Now you have freedom.
Freedom that will last.
Soon it will be all in the past.
Now you have freedom
Freedom at last.

Chapter Four

LET IT BE ME

On the road we traveled, not knowing where we were going. We met an older lady. She was very friendly. She invited us to her home. Her name was Billie. She loved to drink coffee and smoke cigarettes. Her husband also loved to drink coffee and smoke. Gene and I smoked, and drank coffee. So we all got off to a good start. They asked where Gene and I were from. We said Saint Paul, Minnesota. They asked why we were here in California. Gene told Billie and her husband that we were married. We really were only engaged. Billie said that they had a spare room and that we could stay with them. So we stayed with our newfriends.

In a short time, Gene and I got a new place. Gene got a side job singing in a Mexican band. Gene was not popular in California, like he was in Minnesota.

I remained so depressed and homesick. I decided to go back home to my home state Minnesota. In the meantime I met up with a friend named Tony from Minnesota, who now lived in California with his wife and brothernlaw. Tony knew my family. Tony told my parents over the telephone that he would take me to his house and look out for me until I got a plane ticket to get back home to Minnesota. Gene cried and pleaded with me not to leave him, I couldn't say a word. I felt torn inside. I wasn't sure what I should do. If I stayed, I would be homesick. And If I went back to Minnesota, I would be heart broken. A part of me would be missing. I would be missing my first love.

I was making myself feel worse. I wasn't only hurting myself. I was hurting the ones I loved. My second oldest sister said that when I ran away, I broke her trust in me. She said she was mad at me because of the way I had left with my goodbye note. I abandoned my friend Diane, I abandoned my family, I abandoned my dog, I abandoned Gene, my first love. Most important of all, I abandoned the Lord.

Tony took me back to the apartment to get my things. While we were there, we ran into Diane. She was doing well. She had found an apartment with two ladies that were nice to her. She showed us her apartment, it was nice. I wished I could have a nice place like Diane. I thought to myself: Let it be me, Lord. Diane got a job as nurse assistant like we did back in Minnesota. In time Diane became a medical assistant, giving medication to the people that needed it. She was always afraid that she might give the wrong meds to the wrong person, or maybe she would give the wrong dose. She did not want to have that kind of responsibility hanging over her. So she went back to being a nurse's assistant. Over the years Diane had a son named Sam, then a daughter. But she never got married. Not to my knowledge.

LET IT BE ME

Look to me for all of your needs.
Take heed I have my best for you.
You'll know best what next to do.
Take this gesture, try to remember.

I love you, even if you don't surrender.
When you give your heart to me.
It should be clean so let it be me.
As you can plainly see, let it be me.
Could you learn to lean on me?

So please let it be me.
This is what I yearn to learn.
I will draw you near to me.
I have a plan for you and for me.
So please let it be me. It has to be me.
Can you see; in order to be free it has to be me.

I was glad Diane found some nice roommates. I told her I was sorry for what had happened in the past. She said it worked out for the good. If I hadn't done what I did, she would have not met these nice women. I went back to the apartment to get more of my belongings. Gene pleaded with me. He cried and asked me not to leave. He pleaded, "Don't go, don't go, don't leave me." He said we could get a nice apartment, like Diane and her roommates.

I just wanted to go back home. I knew if I went back home to Minnesota, Gene and I could not be together. My dad had previously threatened to hurt Gene. My dad had also threatened Gene, telling him that he better not come back to Minnesota. The day came for me to fly to Minnesota. I was old enough, to move on my own, if I wanted to. Mom and dad never asked any questions. We never talked about the situation.

My cousin Toni tried cheering me up. She arranged a date with a guy friend for me.

He was nice, and we went out. This was the first time I had gone on a date since I have been back to my home state. The man liked to get into fights at the bar. He kept himself under control while I was with him. The man and I went out quite a few times, and we were also intimate with one another, then for personal reasons we both stopped talking and going out together.

My parents did not know what to do to help me. So they had me go to my grandmother's house. My aunt Lupe lived there also. Grandma didn't speak English. I don't think she understood English either. My aunt had to translate everything in Spanish to grandma.

I was still depressed. I just stayed in my room listening to music. Once again I day dreamed. Grandma began to worry that she didn't have enough to feed me, and I had to move back home. I didn't want to move back to my mom and dad's. I felt like a total stranger in my mom and dad's house. When I left my mom and dad's house to go to California, I was a girl. When I came back to Minnesota, I had become a young adult woman.

All my family members were distant from one another. We lived together, yet we were strangers. I felt as though I was misplaced. I felt a sense of misbelonging. I felt strange. How would I feel normal again, or how could I feel accepted, how could I feel that I belonged?

Chapter Five
GET IT TOGETHER

I got a job working at a school doing pottery. This was the place I worked when I was a kid as an art teacher's assistant. It had been a summer school, but turned into a year-round school to give kids a second chance to be able to graduate from high school and get their diploma or GED. This job didn't pay much, but it was a job. I then met up with a friend I knew. She was from New York City, and was real cool. Everyone wanted to be around her. Her name was Susan, and her nick name was Chicky. Chicky said that I could room with her and another gal. The other girl's nickname was Chey. So I did.

I was lucky to be offered a scholarship to go to Normandale college in Bloomington, Minnesota, to attend their Business Secretary program. You had to know more than a regular secretary. It was a three month course and I wouldn't have to pay to go. Sister Giovanni offered me this scholarship. She is also the person whom hired me for the pottery job. She was the main nun, who also started this school for the troubled kids. She loved the Mexican people.

I moved a block away from mom and dad, with Chicky and Chey. I also decided to take sister Giovanni's offer. I took the scholarship and went to school full time. I was doing well. Then Chey started getting drunk and loud. Chey would bring guys in and have sex with them. Chicky and I tried to talk sense to her, but Chey didn't listen to us. We would get high together smoking marijuana. There was this man that came to party with us. He had sex with Chicky. It was her very first time. She was twenty years old. We found out the man was married. Chicky felt bad that her first time was with a married man, but we did not know he was married. Chey and I tried telling Chicky that everything will be okay. We tried comforting Chicky. Nothing we said seemed to help. It would only take time for Chicky to overcome this time in her life.

We began to get complaints from the neighbors. Most of the people who lived in the building were elderly people. The behavior of my roommate Chey was beginning to affect my performance in school. Chey continued to get high. She continued to bring men home to have sex. She continued being loud. We kept getting complaints.

The day came when Chey, Chicky and I got an eviction notice. We each had to find a new place to live. So we decided to go our own ways. We had only lived together a few months. I went to a party and met this African-American guy named Howard. He was very light-skinned. The only way you could tell he was African-American was by his hair. He was a karate teacher. I told him my situation. He helped me find a place to live.

I did not want to tell my parents that I had recently been evicted. I didn't want them to know that I had failed. The only thing at the time I could afford was a duplex apartment in Saint Paul on University Avenue. I would go for walks alone not knowing that I lived in a dangerous neighborhood. Every now and then a vehicle would stop, asking me if I wanted a ride. I would tell them "I'm going for a walk."

Then they would ask, "Do you want to get high?" I would say sure. Sometimes I would get them high.

Now it was Howard's time to find a place to live. Since he had helped me find a place to live, I told him that he could stay with me until he found a place. Howard talked about getting married. I just wanted to be friends. I met his aunt and uncle. They tried telling us that marriage is hard. Howard began getting on my nerves. He would follow me when I left the house. I felt like I was being smothered and I felt like I was suffocating. I needed space, I needed air. If I went on a date, Howard would tag along. To me, Howard and I were just friends. But to him we were more. My mistake was I had sex with him. We were friends with benefits.

I didn't have a phone, so I would walk to the gas station to use the pay phone. The gas station was down at the corner from where I lived. I would call my mom every now and then, just to let her know that I was fine. But in reality, I was running out of money. I was running out of time.

My checks were going to stop. It was only a three month course on my scholarship that I got paid for. I was going to have to find a job, and a better area to live in.

One day I ran into my old roommate Chicky from New York. She was happily with a man and having a baby. I didn't know if they were married or not. I never saw them again. I knew one thing for sure: that I didn't like where I lived at the time. And I didn't like who was staying with me. Howard was getting on my nerves.

I didn't know how I was going to get rid of Howard without being mean. No matter how I put it, I was going to be mean. I couldn't just tell him to leave. It felt wrong to boot him out with no place to stay. But I needed to get away from Howard.

Once when I was out I heard someone calling me. I looked around and saw a white Cadillac with a blue angel on the hood. There were two black men inside the car. The driver called me over to the car. The man asked if I was working. I said no. I didn't know at the time that he meant working the streets. meaning- prostitution. I was green, meaning not street wise. I didn't know that the avenue I lived on was known for drugs and prostitution. The driver asked me if I wanted to get high. I said okay. The driver's name was Phil. The little guy in the back seat was named Warren. Phil said that they just came from California, and they had just come into town after selling their house. Since Howard was getting on my nerves. I decided to hang out with these guys. We got high all right....

I began to experiment with other drugs besides marijuana. I tried a drug called tee similar to the drug speed. Then I tried cocaine. It made me feel so good. I seemed to forget about all my troubles. I felt like I could do whatever I wanted to. I never went back home to my apartment. Whatever happened to Howard? Time went by, and I saw Howard. He was doing okay. He saw me pregnant with Phil's child. We just said our hellos and goodbyes. That was the last time I saw Howard.

GET IT TOGETHER

Get it together, no matter what kind of weather.
Get it together, rise and shine don't waste any time.
If you're feeling weak do not freak, be meek, get it together.
If your plans don't work out, don't be in doubt
Give a shout
Get it together whatever type or doubt or trial
Do not fear of harm be a dear and show your charm.
Get it together no matter what kind of weather,
We will gather together.
Let's get it together, get it together...
There are no grantees for tomorrow so sprees for today,
Don't drown your sorrows get it together; let's get it together.

Chapter Six

RUNNING FROM ONE MAN TO ANOTHER

Phil, Warren and I ended up in a hotel, the Saint Paul hotel. I looked out the window, which was a few stories high, and I felt like jumping out of the window. I felt suicidal. Nobody knew that I felt suicidal. Phil made love to me. Every day I was high from the time I got up until the time I went back to bed, not knowing what was ahead.

Warren looked up to Phil. He wanted to be like him. Warren knew sign language. He was partially deaf. Warren fell in love with me. He says he saw me first, before Phil did.

Phil would try to talk me into prostituting myself on the streets. He wanted me to sell sex. Every day we would just sit in the car getting high. Phil began to talk about working the streets. I couldn't believe it. I told him I couldn't. We sat in the car for hours at a time, getting high. I would keep patting my foot on the car floor. Phil kept trying to persuade me. He tried to convince me that I had sex with guys before. He said, "You were giving it away for free. Why not get paid for it?" Phil continued to sweet talk me.

I didn't really enjoy sex. I only did it for the heck of it. I didn't have orgasms like some women do, although I did experience it one time. I had to take a Valium pill to relax. I couldn't continue taking pills to make me relax just to have an orgasm. Besides, I could only try to enjoy sex with my guy that I was with at the time. I wondered sometimes if I was normal. I seemed to be tense inside, I didn't know how to relax. At times I felt like a robot.

On the other hand, I wanted Phil to be proud of me. The day came when I finally had enough guts to try it. Phil gave me a handful of condoms. I walked down the street. In no time a man stopped and asked if I wanted a date. I said okay. We went to a hotel and I was there only a few minutes. I tuned my feelings out. I also dreaded what I was getting myself into. I got fifty dollars for ten minutes, and Phil was proud of me. When I was done working for the night, I took a shower. To Phil it was as though I was pure again.

When I walked down the streets, I looked sweet and innocent. I didn't dress like a common prostitute. If anything I dressed like a business woman. Men were skeptical to talk to me. Sometimes, I was asked by some men if I were a cop.

I didn't work much. I only did two men a day. It was enough to pay for our daily needs. I did see some prostitutes out all day, freezing their butts in the winter. They had to find some place to warm up. The cops never knew I was a prostitute. I wasn't on the street very long at all.

Phil, Warren and I lived in hotels, and ate at fast food places every day. As long as we had a place to stay, food and our drugs, we were content. Sometimes if the bag of marijuana, we got was no good, Phil would throw it away. Then he would buy a different bag. What I mean by no good is that the marijuana got you sleepy. That's when it was no good. Phil acted like he was a millionaire, wasting marijuana and flashing his money.

Guys like Phil would have a money clip. Then they would get a bunch of ones, then they would put a big bill on top. Like a hundred dollar bill. This made it look like he had a lot of big bills. They would flash their money in front of people to be noticed. Sad but true. This was also a way to get jumped and robbed. You really couldn't flash your money, or you would end up with no money. Then you also end up with some bruises for free along with a bump or two, and maybe some blood with stitches. This is what you get for flashing your money, trying to catch that certain person's attention.

If we went to a restaurant, and Phil did not like the way the food or service was, he would complain and get mad at the cooks and waitress. Frustrated, he would say "Let's go." Nobody else complained. We would get up and follow Phil as we walked out the door. I didn't see Phil pay the bill for the poor service or bad cooking that he said we got. Phil would just say, let's go. We got up and followed Phil out of the restaurant, no questions asked.

One morning Phil ate a cinnamon sweet roll with a piece of salami luncheon meat on top. With chocolate milk. It sounds disgusting. Surprisingly, it was very tasty. It was good.

Sometimes Phil would go gambling at someone's house. One day, Phil came back from gambling. He was very, very upset. He had lost six to eight hundred dollars. Once I went with him to watch him gamble dice. The guys got mad at each other and pulled out guns on each other in front of me. This was crazy. And dangerous. It wasn't safe for me to be there. In fact it wasn't safe for Phil to be there. If he won money instead of losing it, then that's okay. But there was no guarantee that Phil would win. On the other hand, if Phil won, he could get shot at by the other guy that lost his money. So in the long run, there is no winner. That was the first and last time Phil took me with him to watch him gamble.

One night Phil took me to his friend's house in Saint Paul. He said to wait for him there. He said he had some business to take care of, and he would be back. Meanwhile, his friend tried to rape me. I fought as best I could. I managed to fight this man, and I ran away. I ran out of the house and down the street. I didn't know where I was. I came across this big house. I knocked on the door. A young man opened the door. I asked if I could come inside. There were five or six young men playing pool. I was crying as I told them that a man just tried to rape me. The young men were kind and polite. I couldn't believe they were nice, and polite to me. The young men did not try anything on me that night. I could hardly believe it. They could have done anything to me. Nobody knew where I was. Not even myself. The young men said that I could stay there for the night. It felt like I didn't sleep all night. I could have dozed off for a bit. In the morning, I said thanks, then I was on my way.

Phil was out all night looking for me in his car. He finally found me lost in an alley. I told him what had happened. Phil said his friend had told him I was trying to have sex with him. Phil said, "I knew he was lying." Phil and I drove back to his friend's house. Phil stopped the car. Handing me a handgun, he told me to shoot his friend that had tried to rape me. Phil told me that I could tell the police it was self-defense. I didn't have enough guts to take another person's life. I know that I have done wicked things in my life. But I was not wicked enough to take another person's life. There was no way Phil could talk me into it.

I wished I could have said no to everything Phil wanted me to do. Once, Phil had me open a checking account. Then he had me write multiple bad checks. I wasn't even aware there was no money in the account. Once Phil wanted me to buy him a new wardrobe. I just did what he told me. Phil wanted to get married. He said a lot of women tried to get him to marry them. I went along with it. My family was against me marrying Phil. As usual i rebelled. I usually did the opposite of what i was told.

A preacher married Phil and me at the court house in down town Saint Paul. My older brother and my aunt came to witness Phil and I get married. During the ceremony I wanted to back out of it. Yet I was afraid to say anything, so I went through with it. Later, we ran into a neighbor guy and his fiance. We had told them that we had just gotten married. They invited us to their home for turkey dinner.

Phil would always be thinking. He rarely verbally expressed what he was thinking about. He would keep quiet and keep to himself. He did a lot of thinking. He would tell Warren and me what to do. Then the next thing I know Phil was talking me into working for a Minnesota escort agency.

I couldn't believe he wanted me to work for an escort service. Again, he talked me into it.

I learned how the agency worked. The agency supplied me with a pager. I would stop at the closest pay phone and check in. Cell phones were not invented yet. The escort agency would send me on a call. Phil would drive me there. Most of the time, the men wanted sex. So they would have to pay more money. Phil was my driver.

I then got a job at a Minneapolis sauna that sold sex services. One night two undercover police officers came into the sauna pretending to be customers. Then one of my co-workers screamed "Run, it's the cops!" Minneapolis police took everyone that was at the sauna to jail. Two or three hours later Phil bailed me out.

We met two Caucasian female friends of Warren at their apartment in Minneapolis. They were originally from Buffalo, New York. They were deaf. They spoke sign language. We learned a few street talk words in sign language. For instance, in sign language to say, "the cops," we would put our hand under our chin and wiggle the fingers. That meant the pig's which is the cops. We also learned "little boy" in sign language street talk. You say it by rubbing your nose onto your sleeve, because that's what little boys do when they have a running nose. Phil and I laughed. Some of the sign language street talk was cute. That same night we meet a Caucasian gay man that was deaf. His name was Alex. He was a male prostitute. He was the two deaf girl's friend. At first I was freaked out, because I had never met a gay deaf guy before. In fact I never met a gay man before. There were a lot of things I never saw. I believe this was God protecting me again. This man, he was wearing pink lipstick. And blue eye shadow. He had overly dark eyebrows. His hair was light brown. He had not put on his makeup right that night. He was wearing too much. He looked like a clown. I kept silent and watched the deaf people talk in sign language to one another.

We ended up leaving the deaf girl's apartment. We went to Warren's apartment building in Minneapolis. We were there for a few days. Warren washed our laundry and made fried chicken. One day when I looked out the apartment window, I saw a Minneapolis police vehicle stop and harass a black man. I saw one Caucasian police officer exiting the police vehicle. The police officer physically grabbed the black man walking down the street. He roughly handcuffed him. The police officer hit the man with a black night stick while the man was handcuffed. They roughed up the man, then left. The injured man lay on the ground.

Warren and I usually did what Phil wanted us to do. We looked up to him. Phil was in the process of teaching Warren how to be a pimp. I soon found out that Phil had another lady working for him. She was black and deaf. She also spoke sign language. Her name was Lolita. She had beautiful eyes. They were bluish gray. She also was a prostitute. When I found out about the affair I was mad. Phil tried explaining why Lolita was with him I was upset. If I wasn't going to be the only one then I wanted out. Phil said okay, he would let Lolita go. He didn't need other women. I gave him what he needed and wanted.

Phil had a son in California. His name was Danny. Phil showed me a picture of him once. I wanted a son as well. Danny's mom was Caucasian. Her name was Jenny. Phil told me that Jenny had previously done illegal things for him. Such as, write bad checks. To my knowledge, she didn't prostitute, that's all I knew. Jenny used Phil's last name. I wondered if maybe Jenny was married to him. I really didn't know much about this guy. He could have had a few names. He also could be living more than one identity. As time went on, I would find out more things about Phil.

At times I felt as though I was here in body only. This was the strangest feeling I ever experienced. This same feeling came upon me one more time. When a few of my relatives gave me a bridal shower, before I got married to Phil.

Phil and I found an apartment in Minneapolis. We opened our own escort agency. We called it, "Pure Joy." I pretended that there were three women who worked there. I made up descriptions of three different women. The third lady I described was really my measurements. The men always wanted my measurements. So I took the appointment with the clients. We advertised in the local newspaper. Phil taught me how to talk sexy on the phone. At times I talked tough, so I didn't get any hassles. Phil would hide in the closet, in case I needed his help. Phil was my bodyguard.

One day an elderly Caucasian man in his eighties entered my apartment wanting to know if he could just see what I looked like naked. He wanted to pay by giving me used children's toys, wooden and plastic toy blocks. This is called barter. It means paying with something other than money. Kind of like an exchange or trade.

Phil wanted me to meet some of his family. Two of his brothers lived in Saint Paul. Two lived in Minneapolis. One of Phil's brothers. He had an African-American wife that was years younger than him. They had a few children. They seemed happy. I met another one of Phil's brothers. He was a pimp. He lived in Minneapolis and had a nice house. He had three women living with him who worked for him. Two of the women were Caucasian. One was African American. This woman had a little girl. While I was sitting there at the house the ladies would be staring at me. On a different occasion I met a sister of Phil's. Then Phil took me to meet another brother of his. He seemed to be just an ordinary guy living with his girlfriend. After Phil and I left his brother's house, Phil said that his brother's girlfriend wanted me. I just shook my head. I wasn't going to do out of freaky. No matter how much money was involved. No matter how high I was. I was lucky I never was in a postion to do anything freaky or out of the orderary. I have heard of some things that other women have done. That were not the normal. I feel that God was looking after me even when I was doing w range. Even if I was in danger the Lord was still there. Looking out for me. Protecting me from damage. real harm or even death. Where their was no way for me. God always made a way. I don't understand why me? What did I do to have God's favor. I don't deserve his kindness and goodness. Nor his patience, or his compassion. Even when we don't deserve his love, forgiveness, nor his slow to anger. Yet the Lord stays faithful! in his promises. And in his word. The Lord never gives up on us. Even if we turn our backs on him. The Lord won't give up on us. Just to see a rainbow in the sky. Is *contort* that the Lord will not flood the earth again. Just little things to let me know that he is faithful!. And that his word is powefull and true. Everyday I am reminded that he is alive and that he loves me. Just to tell him that I love him. Makes me feel good and in love with him. Their was a time when I felt the L ordl so close That he felt so real. Almost as if he were human. I wish I could feel that all the time. Yet I feel him so real in different ways. This is awesome and a blessing from the Lord. I wouldn't have it any other way. God's way is best.

RUNNING FROM ONE MAN TO THE NEXT

I could write a text, of an awful hex.
Or the thought of you with your ex.
Perhaps this is lust. Another one bites the dust.
Now I am in disgust, whom do I trust?

Running from one man to another,
Just the thought makes me shutter.
I couldn't even tell my mother.
When all else fails. I keep it to myself.
Not telling anyone else.

Running from one man to another,
I have you lord to tell.
Hell will make you yell!
This is not a fairy tale.
Now I am in demand.

So take my hand, I will take a stand.
I don't have to run from no man.
Because Jesus is the man! He has
A special plan. For your life span.

I have to stop running from one man to the next
Then things won't be so perplexed.
I have to stop running from one man to the next.
I am running from one man to the next.
What's going to happen next? I am perplexed.

Running from one man to the next.
When will I stop running from one man to the next?
Why do things have to be so perplexed?
Perhaps this is such a hex
What am I to do next?

Chapter Seven

DANCE, DANCE, DANCE

Phil brought a young woman home. Her name was Cathy. She was an alcoholic. We helped her recover from drinking. We gave her a job escorting for our agency. When Cathy went on a call, men didn't want her. I guess she wasn't pretty enough. I had to cover for her. I was stuck doing everything. I was mad. Cathy was more bother than she was worth. It seemed Cathy couldn't do anything right. Cathy couldn't answer the telephone right. Cathy said at one time that she danced in a club. So Phil had Cathy audition at a club. She was hired. When she danced, she had the biggest smile you ever did see. She was happy up on the stage, dancing for the customers, and taking off her clothes.

Phil and I got high on marijuana and cocaine. Then Phil and Cathy began persuading me into auditioning for the nightclub. Taking my clothes off for many strangers, I couldn't do it. I couldn't bring myself to do it. But Phil was persuasive, and after a time, I decided to give it a try.

When it was my turn to audition. I began dancing sexy. I looked out at the audience and got shy and scared. I ran off the stage. Phil didn't get mad with me. Phil continued persuading me to audition again. I decided to give it another try. I went through with the audition and I was hired. Phil and Cathy were proud of me. We worked at the night club for a few months. I used the stage name of Sexy Sandy. Phil gave me a big costume, ring with the letter "S," my stage name initial, in diamonds. I doubted they were real diamonds. But the ring was very pretty.

DANCE, DANCE, DANCE

I used to dance for man, now I am in
demand so please take my hand. When I think
of the kingdom, I know that I have freedom.
When I feel free, I know I can be me. So I
look to the heavens. Dancing one to eleven.
I am not going to take a chance. That this
might be my last. Chance too dance. I will be in

a trance, when I am in romance and I'll dance and
dance so I keep in romance. I will give you another
chance. It will be no bother go into a trance and dance.
For this is your chance. I am dancing for my Lord.
I need to be on the right cord. For me and for my Lord.
At times I feel like I am flying in the air. Now I do not
need to be in despair. I feel as if the Lord has me in his arms,

he has showed me some of his charms. In a trance
I dance here on earth. Dreaming by the hearth.
Soon I'll be in heaven's birth. I will dance for,
eternity. Just the Lord and me. For all to see.
Open your eyes you will plainly see.
That I am dancing, the Lord and me.
For all to see, take my word of accord,
you won't be bored. Sometimes I feel like
I am a flying cord. This is my last chance.
I am not lying. There's no denying.
I just have too dance. Come on take
a chance so dance, dance, dance.

Running into the arms of Love

Cathy and I were hired by a dance agency. They were originally from Minnesota. This agency had us travel to different night clubs on a weekly basis. The agency once sent us to Fargo, North Dakota. Phil, Cathy and I drove to Fargo. The weather was bad. There was a blizzard. The snow was very deep. The temperature was below zero. Phil and Cathy got sick. They had to be on prescription cough medicine. Shortly after the visit to Fargo, Cathy and I quit.

We all decided that we would drive to California. Cathy and I soon got a job at a night club dancing and serving drinks. Employees at the club frequently would get high and drunk I remembered seeing different drama instances. One woman was sneaking up on the bouncer. She wanted to get revenge. I don't know what the bouncer did or said to make her mad, and so mean. She wanted to hurt this man. One woman got so drunk, she was staggering. She could not perform properly. A middle aged guy convinced me to buy a drug. He said it was angel dust. I'd never had angel dust before. I think it was an acid pill. I bought the pill from him, and took it backstage in one of the shared dressing rooms behind the big curtain. That's were many of us, if not all of us, women did drugs and alcohol.

When I got back to the hotel that night, I was delusional. I was lying on a hotel bed. I closed my eyes. I saw things that were happening that actually weren't happening at the moment. I saw my grandmother in a wheelchair. In reality, she wasn't. I saw a severe snow storm in California. I then began to shake on the hotel bed. The television was on. I heard people laughing on the television. I thought they were laughing at me. I thought they were making fun of me for being such a fool, taking drugs from a stranger. The acid pill was a negative experience for me. I decided never to take street drugs from a stranger. It was a foolish thing I did.

Once in a while, famous men would come into the club. They would grade our dancing. Sometimes they would offer dancers parts in movies or tv shows. Or they would offer us engagements for private parties for celebrities. Fame for a little while. One of my co-workers got a part on the Lavern and Shirley show. One day a man offered us women a try out for a part in a movie about cheerleaders. There were three positions available to try out for. One leading part and two other parts. Around this time Alex Gibbs came into the club and asked if a few of us ladies wanted to dance at a private party for singer Marvin Gaye's surprise birthday party. The singer Michael Jackson was also to be there. Alex Gibbs gave three of us ladies his business card.

So I went back to the hotel and showed Phil the business card I was given from Mr. Gibbs. Phil got excited. I had not known who Alex Gibbs was. Phil handed me an album showing me his name on back as producer. Phil said, now we are big timing. I never went to audition with Alex Gibbs.

One dark night Cathy, Phil and I were driving in a car. Phil said he had to take care of some business. Phil meets up with a man whom I never seen before. It was very dark, so it was hard to see what he really looked like. The man was black and a big husky guy. It seemed this man was having a hard time keeping his balance. I think this man was drunk or high. Phil got out of the car and began talking with this man. Cathy was in the back seat, and I was up front. Phil went in back of the car we were riding in. He was talking with the man. Phil came back to the front of the car. He was upset. The man and Phil had a disagreement. Then Phil said we were going to give the man a ride somewhere. The man got in the back seat with Cathy.

From what I remember hearing the man was slurring his words. Meanwhile Phil was driving and it was dark. The man continued slurring his words. He said he wanted out of the car I turned around to see why the man wanted to get out of the car. I turned around and I saw Cathy firmly holding onto the man. Phil stopped the car, on the side of the road. He turned around from the driver's side of the car. He then looked back at the man and Cathy. Cathy was still hanging onto the man so he wouldn't get out of the car. Phil took a hidden handgun. Then he shot the man in the upper stomach or chest. The man made a painful groaning sound. Cathy then pushed and shoved the man, she was having a hard time getting this man out of the car because she was skinny, and too weak. Phil had to help her get the guy out of the car. The whole time I was screaming and crying. They managed to get the guy out of the car. Then they rolled him down a big hill on the side of the road. I kept screaming and crying. I couldn't stop crying and afterwards Phil, Cathy and I went to a hotel. It was a nice place.

Something happened to me. I wouldn't eat I wouldn't talk. I became a mute. I remained like a zombie. I was just here in body and the rest of me was not. I was totally out of it. I do remember going from one hospital to another. Nobody knew what was wrong with me. The nurse asked me for my telephone number. I finally spoke a few words. I gave her my social security number. Instead of my phone number. Phil got upset with the people, he said to them can't you see she doesn't know anything, she's out of it. Then we went to two more hospitals. We could not get any answers. So we went to a hotel for the rest of the night. Once again I was like a zombie. We were trying to find out what was wrong with me. We couldn't get any answers from the people at every hospital I went to.

I went outside the next day. I looked up at the sun trying to blind my eyes. For some reason I was trying make my eyes go blind. There were moments when I couldn't stop crying. I believe I had a temporary nervous breakdown. All I did was cry, cry, and cry.

The three of us moved to a different hotel every couple of days. I didn't know why we didn't stay at one place for too long. In time I realized the reason why we kept moving every few days. It was because Phil and Cathy killed a man. So they had to keep moving in order to flee the cops. We ended up in Las Vegas. I started to hear my dad's voice. He was saying my nick name, Tiny. He was saying. "Tiny run, run Tiny, go." I didn't know where to run. Or where to go.

I continued to cry and cry. One night Phil and Cathy went out to get some fast food. When they returned, Phil said to me "I'm tired of seeing you cry." Then he told me I didn't have to work anymore. Then handed me a drink of soda. I took one drink I looked up at Phil and Cathy. They looked like devils. I went into shock. They called the paramedics.

One of the male medics came in sarcastically laughing, asking Phil, "What is she on?" Phil said nothing. Maybe Phil and Cathy wanted me dead so they would not have to worry about me if I started to talk again. Then I wouldn't tell the police what I saw happen. Maybe they wanted me out of the picture so Phil and Cathy could be together as well. Or maybe they wanted to get rid of me. Maybe I was just no use to them if I wasn't working and making money.

I could hear everything and see everything I just could not respond. Then the medics put smelling salt, under my nose. I popped up like a jack in the box. I was taken in the ambulance to one hospital after another. Nobody knew what was wrong with me. Eventually I sneaked out of the hospital. I was wandering around and did not know where I was.

A black man picked me up, took me to his house, and made love to me. He said all I needed was some T. L. C. I didn't know at the time, he meant Tender, Loving, Care. I was like a zombie. I just stared. I watched the man take off his condom filled with sperm and flushed it down the toilet. Then I looked in the mirror, and wondered. Who was I? We really didn't talk. In fact when the man was making love to me, I thought he was phil. So I said to the man, Phil? The man just kept silent. When we were done the man let me go. Where? I didn't know where to go. I was wondering around aimlessly like a fugitive. I felt all alone and scared. I didn't know who to trust. Or if I could trust. I didn't know anybody or anything.

After a long time, a policeman picked me up. He laughed at me. This policeman looked like my uncle back in Minnesota. Next thing I knew I was in a state hospital. They called me Jane Doe. They drugged me until my eyes were dilated. I saw them force a big guy to take a shot. He was screaming as they held him down and forced him to take a shot. There was this woman, who had red hair and big blue eyes. We became friends. Everyone wanted to be around us. They followed us around. They gave us their money to buy stuff from the canteen. The red head did the math.

About three months later, I began to talk. This was progress. I finally remembered my name. I also remembered that I had a family. I remembered their telephone number. I called my grandma, and she said that Phil had called looking for me. She told me that Phil told her that I had a brain tumor. This was not the truth. There was a nurse in this place that looked just like my aunt back in Minnesota. I must have been homesick. When I called my mother and told her that I had seen Phil and Cathy kill a guy. I had forgotten about it. I must have blocked it out of my mind as I did other things. Phil found me again. Phil always found me. I talked to Phil on the phone. I told him to come and get me out of there. So Phil came to my rescue, or so I thought. Phil and I drove back to Minnesota. We never saw Cathy again.

Chapter Eight

ANTICIPATING MY FIRST BORN

We drove back to Saint Paul. Back in Minnesota, Phil and I picked up one of his brothers. Phil let his brother drive the car. We got high while Phil made love to me in the back seat. Then Phill and his brother had business to do. Shortly after, Phil and I got an apartment in Minneapolis. It was a nice place, a one bedroom only a block from the police station. I began to feel sick to my stomach. Yet I was hungry. So I made myself a sandwich. I felt it go halfway down. Then it came right back up. Then I realized I hadn't had my period for a while. If I'm pregnant it had to have happened in the back seat of the car. Phil and I thought that I should go to the doctor. Then I found out that I was pregnant. I was happy. I had wanted a baby since I was seventeen. I was happy, but also scared. I believed this was not the right time to have a baby. Phil was pressuring me to get an abortion. I didn't believe in abortion. This baby was a living being.

Phil began hitting me. He said if I didn't get an abortion, that he would kick the baby out of my stomach. I knew that I had to protect my baby and myself. He began throwing lit cigarettes on me. He also whipped me with a telephone cord. He wanted me to work the streets. I refused. Phil sent me out to work. All I did was sit at a bus stop. Phil yelled at me saying that I looked terrible, that I needed to put some make up on. Then I called my mom and told her that Phil was trying to make me prostitute and that I was pregnant. Mom said, "Come home." I will never forget those words. I couldn't believe that mom said to come home. I never thought in my wildest dreams that mom would still accept me back into her home. I guess I felt that I would be rejected after they knew what I had done with my life. I felt embarrassed and ashamed for the wicked lifestyle I had been living.

It took many years for me to learn to forgive myself and to learn to not be ashamed or feel guilty. Because God had forgiven me of all, not some but all, my sins. And remembered my sins no more. I had to forgive and forget as well. All along all I had to do was call my family. So I waited until Phil went to sleep. It was about two in the morning. I crawled out the window and ran to the police station. I told them about my situation. They took me to my parent's home. There I felt safe. I was around family. This meant a great deal to me. I never knew that family can be so important. I needed some support. After all I was going to be a mother. During holidays I always felt like crying, because just having family was a great feeling. This was very comforting. This was very important to me. It was a touching time for me. Having family meant a lot to me. It meant everything to me.

I'VE BEEN WAITING FOR YOU

I've been waiting for this moment for so long,
To want to hold you and cuddle you all day long.
I've been waiting so long, here in my tummy is
where you belong, I've been waiting for you for so long.
I'll wait a few months longer, before you come along.

I've been waiting for so long. Soon it won't be long.
You'll be in my arms for this is where you belong.
Safe in my arms is where you belong. I've been, waiting
for so long. I've been waiting for so long, to hold you
in my arms. I will do you no harm. I can't wait until

Running into the arms of Love

you are in my arms I've been waiting waiting for so long.
Come to me my sweet child where you belong I've been
waiting, waiting for so long. I want to sing you a song.
For so long. Don't worry you will have love and security.
Come to me my sweet child of mine. I've been waiting for so long.

I began to show. I needed maternity clothes. So I went to the store and got a few things. The whole nine months I felt depressed. I was on bed rest. The Doctor did not put me on bed rest, my depression did. All day I laid on the bed, I just watched daytime television. That was my life. I lived upstairs in my mom and dad's duplex home. My aunt Lisa took child birth classes with me. At least I would not be alone for the birth of my baby. I felt sad that Phil wasn't around to experience the birth of his son. I had to realize that Phil didn't want any part of this. I did have family around. For this I was grateful.

I was glad that I lived in the same state as the rest of my family. It was a good feeling having relatives in the same state. Even if we didn't see each other, or talk to one another on a regular basis. Once in a while I would run into a cousin at a store. I began to get bigger as the months flew by. Then one day I fell down the stairs at my mom's house. I plopped and bounced down each step. I landed on my rear end. My mom got scared, she came running to help me up. I was shaken up. Mom gave me a glass of water and asked if I was okay. It took a little while to calm down, but I was okay. I was glad the baby was all right.

On payday mom and I walked down to the Brown Derby bar. They had good burgers and fries. I was on welfare. I liked to treat mom to lunch and buy her something she wanted. This time I wasn't trying to buy love. I wanted to do it because it was fun. Every day I would look around my duplex. I frequently talked to God. I knew He was real. Somehow I knew He was watching over me. I went to church with my grandma. She was a Catholic. So was I. I continued to talk to God on an individual basis. I thanked him every day for all I had.

One night I was taking a bath. I lay in the tub and relaxed for a little while. I didn't want to get out of the tub. My parents' home was drafty. So I put a little electric heater on to try to stay warm it was so nice and warm under the water. As I was getting out of the tub and wiping myself dry, I felt funny. I felt different.

I began getting sharp pains. I began to wonder if my water broke while I was in the bathtub. I called my aunt. She said yes, I was going into labor. She said she would be on her way to pick me up and go to the hospital.

I had a hard labor. Every time my cervix got to a centimeter, it would be stuck there for hours. This was a long process. I was having a hard time. I had long hair; it was in a ponytail. I wanted to rip my hair out. I knew I was going to have a boy. The desire of my heart. However, this was taking too long. I was in labor approximately twenty-two hours. My baby finally came out. When he cried, it sounded like he said, "Ma."

Everyone said, "Awwww! He said ma!" We all laughed. Later when I was back in the room, the baby was cleaned up. They brought my baby to me. As I was holding him I thought to myself what I would name him. I never even thought of a name for the baby. The name Tod popped in my head. So I said to the baby as he was looking at me, I think I'll call you Tod. The baby just smiled as if he agreed with me. Todd did smile a lot.

The woman I shared a room with at the hospital had a newborn boy as well. She never told me she was a Christian until we both were leaving the hospital. The women I shared a room with asked me to promise her something. I said, "What?"

She said, "Promise me you will find a church and go to it." I said okay.

I took my baby home. He was only six pounds. Twenty two and a half inches long. How could a little guy like him cause so much pain? When I brought my new baby home, my dad said, "Look at the little peanut." I loved my baby. My baby didn't seem satisfied. He wanted to eat all the time. All he wanted to do was eat, if he wasn't sleeping. I was breastfeeding him. I didn't know if I was doing right. All I had to do was keep feeding him until he was satisfied. I didn't know what to do because mom never breastfed any of us kids. So I didn't think I was doing a good job breastfeeding. So I gave him a bottle. Mom said put a little cereal in his bottle of milk. Then slit the bottle nipple. So the cereal could come out with the milk. So I did what mom told me. My baby seemed more content. Then he got diarrhea bad. He had to go into the hospital. I could hear my baby. He wasn't in his bassinet. He was still at the hospital. I felt empty without my baby. Tod was in the hospital a day or two. It seemed longer. I missed my baby. I could hear the sounds Todd made.

Little Tod came home. I was glad, my baby was well and home. They put Tod on soy bean milk. Pediatricians said he needed that kind of milk. I forgot to tell the Doctors that I gave him baby cereal, maybe that's why he got diarrhea. He was too young to have cereal. I didn't think about it until later.

I decided I would try to get a job. I looked in the paper. There was an opening at a veterinarian. So I applied and got an interview. I think I dressed too fancy for the place I was applying a job for. I should have dressed casual. I felt out of place. I didn't get the job. I felt disappointed. I wanted to get off welfare. I wanted to support my son and me. I didn't want the government supporting us.

I wanted Phil to see his son. Phil had moved back to California. He came to Minnesota for his mom's funeral. Todd and I met up with Phil I never did meet Phil's mom while she was alive. Phil pretended to cry. He wasn't a very good actor. You could tell he was faking, there were no tears. We were at his family's gathering. Everyone was in the kitchen and living room, but Phil and I were on the staircase. Then Phil began to choke me. I couldn't scream for help. Phil wanted us to get back together. I said I'm not sure, I needed more time. I didn't know what I was going to do. We agreed that he would stay with me until after the funeral. So Phil stayed with me and the baby while he was in town. I met a sister of his. She loved Tod. But nobody loved Tod, more than me. Except Jesus of course. While Phil was in town he would attempt to take control of my welfare money. He tried to get me to work the streets again. I became a nervous wreck. I felt like Phil was trying to take control of my money, and my life.

If we went out I paid my mom to baby-sit Tod. Later my mom said if she would have known that I was the one paying her she wouldn't have taken the money. She thought Phil was paying her money.

Tod needed a crib. So we looked in the newspaper. Phil found a used crib at a garage sale. I was mad that Phil had bought a used crib. I was sad. I wanted us to be a real family. I wanted Tod to have his own father. Yet, I was only fantasizing. I knew that's not what Phil wanted. I was hoping that Phil would change. I wanted him to be like his brother that had a lovely home and family. This was wishful thinking.

I would continue talking to the Lord. I would also listen to my radio at night. During the day I would watch television, the soaps, like when I was pregnant. When I talked to Phil on the phone. I told him I was going to church. He told me to stop going to church and to stop praying. He would try to talk me into going back with him to California. Phil would say what kind of life is that for me, listening to the radio and being lonesome. I continued talking to God anyhow.

Chapter Nine

ONE WAY TICKET TO HELL

Phil and I continued to talk long distance, on the telephone. Phil mailed me a one-way airplane ticket to California. In the meantime I prayed to the Lord, asking him what I should do. I asked the Lord for a sign. I said, "Please, God, give me a sign. Tell me what I should do." The night I was supposed to fly to California, all the flights were canceled because of heavy fog. I believe that was my sign from God that I asked for. Yet, I ignored it. I had forgotten that I asked God for a sign. I rescheduled, not thinking twice about it. I was still a little unsure as to what I was doing to my and my son's lives.

I said my goodbyes. My baby got to go on the airplane free. I was crying. I had to leave my family, to reunite my family. My baby was patting the airplane window, with both his hands. He was amazed, looking at the floating clouds as we passed by. On the airplane ride I was unsure what I was getting myself into. I was not just making decisions, for myself any more. Now I had another person to take care of.

Once I got to California, Phil told me, "This will be the last time I leave him." I wasn't sure what he meant by this remark. I didn't know if it was a threat, or just a statement. When I got to California, Phil told me to go down to the county and apply for assistance. Then He had me get a job in a night club. Phil usually would stay home and take care of Tod, while

I worked at the club. When I wasn't working I took care of Tod We lived in a hotel. We ate fast food every day for breakfast, lunch and dinner. Phil and I took Tod to the park to play a few times. A few little girls would surround Tod, dancing around in a circle like ring-around-the-rosie. They wanted to play with him. Tod was a little charmer. We got to stay at a friends apartment. For a few months. Because the friend was never home.

One day Phil could not babysit Tod. There was this older couple that lived next door to us. We barely knew them. I asked this older couple if they could watch Tod so they did. I let them babysit Tod one time. A few weeks later I saw the woman crying. She told me they were being evicted out of their apartment. They couldn't pay their rent. I believe they were alcoholics. If I had known that they were alcoholics I would not have asked them to babysit my baby. They were decent people. They kept to themselves. I did trust them even if I didn't know them well enough. I still felt bad for them. And I wished there was something I could do to help them. At this time I was trying to help myself.

My world was upside down. I couldn't help being nervous and afraid. It seems I had lived in fear for so long. Fear for many different reasons. Fear of what lies ahead. Fear for my life. There were a lot of ways I could be killed. The devil was always trying to destroy me and kill me. The Lord was always there for me. I didn't know it. In a sense I knew that God heard me talking to him. And for some reason He listened. And the Lord did answer me even when I didn't know it. At times He felt so real and near to me. Yet I didn't seem to make the right choices or decisions for my life. I kept going in the opposite direction that I should have been going in. I think that this was rebellion and stubbornness rolled up into one.

One day Phil brought this young woman to our hotel room. She had been walking and wandering around the streets. She told us she had recently broken up with her boyfriend because he was trying to pimp her. The young woman only stayed with us at the hotel for a couple of days. Then she left to go back to her boyfriend while I was in the bath room. My baby and this women had disappeared. I couldn't find my baby.

I panicked. I started crying and screaming for Tod. He was nowhere to be found. The California police were called. They were out looking for him. All I did was cry, and cry. I cried so much my voice went away. I kept wondering if Tod was crying for me. I didn't know where he was. I couldn't help him. My baby had been kidnapped.

Two days later the police found my baby safe with the young lady. She had bought Tod a short outfit. She was pretending that Tod was her baby. The police said I could press criminal charges on the young woman. When I saw how she loved my son, I couldn't press criminal charges. My heart went out to the young lady. Later, I thought to myself if I had pressed criminal charges, perhaps the young lady would never do this horrible thing to someone else. But I believe deep down I did the right thing.

Things began to get more difficult between Phil and myself. I would cry. Phil would be gone all night, every night. There was something wrong. I believe he was with another woman. In time I found out that Phil was living a double life with both me and another woman named Jenny. The women that he had a son with.

Phil began physically abusing me. Once Phil hit me on the middle of my back, hard enough to leave his handprint on my back. I could not go to work with a hand print on my back. Meanwhile, I also hurt my knee. I had to wear an ace bandage. Now I had to be out of work longer. I didn't know why Phil was getting abusive with me. Whatever night life he was living began to affect his behavior. It was not safe for my baby and me to stay. Phil tried hurting my baby. Every night I cried, because Phil was mistreating me and gone every night. When he was around he was very ornery and short temperd. While Phil was in prison, many years after our divorce, he married Jenny. Then she would go visit him and have sex. Jenny's sons joked around and said that she got pregnant from the guy that drove her to visit Phil. She did not like that kind of joking around. Jenny did not think it was funny. Phil was originally sent to one prison then got transferred to another. He also got out earlier than his original sentence, because of good behavior.

Phil got angry for some reason. He started to grab the baby. I wasn't going to let him hurt my baby. I would do whatever I had to do to keep Tod safe. I jumped on Phil, and started hitting him. I told him he wasn't going to touch the baby. Phil became more and more aggressive and disrespectful towards me. I told a coworker of mine named Jan about my troubles with Phil. Jan said that my son and I could stay with her at her parents' house. My heart was pounding, so fast. I was afraid. If Phil came back while the baby and I were trying to leave, what would he do? I was scared. I had to make a decision. Soon. Because things were getting worse with Phil. I didn't trust him to take care of Tod since he became abusive. I didn't want my baby to be hurt in any way.

ONE WAY TICKET TO HELL

One way ticket to hell,
This is the day, when I can
honestly say, I have a one way ticket.
A one way ticket to hell,
It makes me want to yell,

One way ticket to hell,
Once I go I can never come back.
I have let the enemy take my back.
Now I am under attack. How I would
love to get back on track.

Situation too hard to spell;
One way ticket to hell.
Does that ring a bell?
I could scream... Am I in a fancy dream?

I can't tell; One way ticket to hell.
You will just want to yell. When you become
pale don't worry I won't tell. One way ticket
to hell. Can't tell, oh well; One way ticket to hell.

Chapter Ten

GLIMPSES OF MY LIFE

I knew I had to get away. My baby and I. I wasn't sure if this was the moment I should sneak away from Phil. While Phil was gone, I decided to take my friend's offer to stay with her and her parents. My heart was pounding hard and fast.
At this time I was a walking skeleton. I weighed only eighty-nine pounds. I consumed cocaine and marijuana. On a regularbasis all day long. I also drank alcohol at work. I couldn't eat, I couldn't sleep. The life I wanted to live was not possible. It was only a fantacy. My family was far away from me. I believe isolating me from my family is one of the reasons why Phil brought me out to California. Now I was stuck.

I didn't know how to get my son and myself to safety. I knew I had to act fast. I looked up on the door frame, and there was this picture of Jesus. On the back of the picture was a beautiful prayer. It sounded something similar to this: "Jesus when my hands hurt and I cannot work, Jesus, help me. When I am weak and tired, Jesus, help me." The prayer went on and on. It was by reading this prayer that I became saved.

The Bible says in Joel 2: 32 "Whoever calls upon the name of the Lord shall be saved." I didn't know anything about the Bible, salvation, or prayer. At this very moment, it felt like something happened to me. I believe my heart was transformed from beast to beauty. I Believe Jesus came into my heart. I didn't know any christans. I was on my own all alone. Then I remmbered the women I met in the hospital in how she wanted me to find home church, and go to it. I tried to get into a church next door. Every time I tried to get into this church, it was locked. I didn't see any activity there to my knowledge. I didn't know if this church was vacant. I never saw any people around.

Eventually, I got enough nerve to leave Phil. I gathered a few things of Tod's and mine. We moved to my friend Jan's parent's house located in Culver City, California. I continued to work at the club so I could earn money for a plane ticket back to Minnesota. Meanwhile, Phil would send men into the club with notes for me to meet with him and to see the baby. I refused. The notes kept coming. Then he had a policeman come into the club. I ran behind the curtains and waited until he left. I wondered what lies Phil had told them. My baby and I stayed with Jan and her parents for a few days.

July, 22nd 1980: I will never forget this date as long as I live. This is the day that God saved me from burning in hell and gave me a chance to clean up my life. Phil called me at Jan's parent's house. I don't know how he got the number. Phil asked me to pick a vehicle up and asked if he could see the baby. I asked Jan, her mother Martha, and another woman friend named Barbara if they would go along with me. On the telephone I finally agreed to meet with Phil. When all three of us ladies got to Phil's residence, I took Tod to meet Phil at the screen door of the house. I went inside with Phil and the baby for about twenty minutes while my friends waited outside in the car. Twenty minutes later, I went back to the car where the women were. Phil followed close behind me holding the baby. All along, Phil had a handgun hidden inside the front waistband of his pants.

The whole time, I had this horrible feeling inside of me. I felt like something terrible was about to happen. Its like my heart was going to jump out of my chest. My heart was pounding so fast and hard. I told Phil I wanted to leave, then I reached out for my baby. Phil would not allow me to have him. A slight tugging match took place. Tod began to cry. Finally, I took the baby from Phil's arms and walked away. Phil pulled out a gun, a .38 caliber snub nose revolver. While I was still holding my baby, he pointed the handgun at me with no comment. I was furious that he would point a gun at me, so I shouted at him, "Go ahead and shoot!" Phil pulled the trigger and began shooting the gun. The last thing I saw was him pointing the gun at me. I dropped my baby on the cement, rolled over on my side and fell unconscious. Landing on top of my baby, blackness was the last thing i rember.

Next, Phil walked several feet over to the blue Chevy. He aimed the handgun into the car at my two girlfriends. He fired a shot at Jan's mother, Martha, grazing the back of Martha's head. As Martha fought to stay conscious, Jan attempted to get out of the car and help me. Phil fired a third shot, shooting Jan in the neck as she fell to the ground with a through and through bullet wound. After the third shot, Barbara ran for it. Phil attempted to fire a fourth shot in her direction as Barbra ran around the corner. She wasn't hurt, but she was hysterical. Phil had gone nuts.

With vomit on her purple blouse Barbara ran to an unknown residence. She used their phone to call the Lennox Sheriff's department station regarding the shooting incident. Los Angeles investigators contacted the homicide unit. I was transferred via ambulance and listed in critical condition. I was then taken to Hawthorn community hospital. My physician, Dr. Thompson advised investigators that he had given me forty-eight hours to live. He also added that if I lived more than forty-eight hours I would remain a vegetable for the rest of my life in a comatose state.

With no available family or relatives to care for Tod, the county department of social services took custody of my baby. They placed him in a Los Angeles county shelter home and later transferred him to a county foster home. What had I done to our lives?

I had one surgery to get the bullet out. On first attempt doctors could not locate the bullet. During the second surgery, I got a very bad infection where the bullet entered due to the lead in the bullet. Doctors said I would not survive the surgery. They said I was too weak. Yet the Lord gave me strength. I knew that I would be okay. Although I was not aware of what was really going on, I kept a smile on my face. I was sure that I was going to be okay.

Rachel Tejeda Morris

GLIMPSES OF MY LIFE

There was a time in my life, when I was in strife.
Flashing glimpses, pieces of my life. Like a serrated
knife. Now I know I have to get on with my life.
So remembering the past no more. Now is the time
to let things go. Being content of what
little time we may have spent. Seemingly a dream

like picture. Looking ahead to the future.
Covering-up the bad. In reality it just made me
sad or mad. Glimpses of flash backs.
What's happened to me? I wish I could
push them far as can be. Glimpses of flash

backs that aren't worth a dime.
Glimpses that are lasting and one of a
kind. Now I just want to resign I'll just
take my time. It's worth more than a dime.
I have to stop being in denial.

It seems worthwhile. Then I could smile
a little while longer. This helps make
me stronger. Then again this is only a glimpse
of my life. I began to think twice. I had been
given a chance to start life over again. I feel
like I have been cut up with a serrated knife.
I am in complete strife.

Where do I begin all over again?
Because this is not the end. It's only
the beginning. For a life of less
strife when I think about it twice then
I realize I have been bought with a price.
I think that's all fully nice. A glimpse of
my life with no more strife.

Chapter Eleven

I STAND IN AWE

A week later, I woke up out of a coma. I was flat on my back. I was helpless. I couldn't walk, I couldn't talk and I couldn't do anything. While I was on my death bed, I felt this tremendous, intense heat, as though I was burning up. I looked up and saw an image which looked like the Lord. Although I could not see his face, I knew it was the Lord. At first I got scared, and then in my heart I knew I shouldn't be afraid. The Lord spoke to my heart, saying that I was going to be allright. The Lord sat in a chair next to my hospital bed, for a few seconds, then opened a big, thick book. I thought it was a Bible. Now I believe it was the book of life.

Revelations chapter 20:11- 12 reads: "I saw a great white throne and him who sat upon it, from whose presence, earth and heaven fled away, and no place was found for them and I saw the dead. The great and the small, standing before the throne, and books were opened." Another book was opened. This is the book of life. The dead were judged from the things which were written in the books, according to their deeds.

The Lord's description, to me, was like a shadow, with medium length, wavy hair. He seemed to be wearing a gown. Then the Lord left as miraculously as he had come. During the days that followed, I began to have miracle after miracle happen to me. I believe the vision I had of the Lord was real, and that the book the Lord was holding, symbolized the book of life. Now I know the whole vision that I got from the Lord. Not only is my name written in the book of life. It also means healing. And Healing brings life. So therefore I need to be a part of the healing rooms. What an awesome God.

There was a period of time that I was out of control. The right side of my body was out of control. I had to be tied to the bed. I believe that I was going through withdrawal due to going cold turkey from drugs. I do not remember anything, I only noticed marks around my ankles. So I asked why I had marks around my ankles. My mother told me that the staff had to tie me to the bed.

The Los Angeles police swat team caught Phil at Jenny's house. This is where he was staying at night, living a double life. As time progressed I began to find out more things about Phil. He was living more than one identity. So my assumption was right about Phil

I STAND IN AWE

To have things happen to you.
To have things happen before your very eyes.
It's a great awesome surprise.
To be recognized and theorized.
As a child of God, I stand in awe.
For this is an awesome, awesome sunrise.

I have to look forward and emphasize.
I stand in awe, looking forward to the final prize.
For it cannot be forever in disguise.
Take this from the wise.
I stand in awe, giving my Lord applause.
Looking forward to spas and paradise.

Running into the arms of Love

In the meantime I stand in awe...
clinging to the promises and all.
That the kingdom will be a ball;
and all too tall for you all.
In the meantime I stand in awe.

Waiting for you all. So be a doll and don't fall.
Began to take this all. For I stand in awe.
It's okay to lift your eye brows and then
I know you stand in awe; for I stand in awe.

One day, my pinky finger moved. Soon after that I moved my hand. Every day there seemed to be progress. Miracles, wonders, and works kept happening. I had decided to surrender my all to the Lord. I decided to live the rest of my life serving the Lord. Every day I had people coming to visit me, reading their Bibles. They had heard I had seen a vision of the Lord. People I didn't know came to visit me. Some others brought a little booklet called the Daily Word. I became a prayer warrior.

The head injury results were like having a stroke. My right eye was blinded. My eye was closed shut, and I could not open it. Over the years my right eye has been through heck. The doctor ordered artificial tear drops to be put in my eye. My eye evenually opened up. Then I got an infection. So I had to have surgery to close my eye lid to protect my eye. After surgery it looked like I had a droopy eye lid. My eye lid was a Band-Aid for my eye. Then my eye started to hurt and pain. This was horrible. Eventually the doctors decided to remove my eyeball. After that I needed a fake eye. I used whatever was available, even if the color did not match my other eye. I had to get special permission from the state to get a prosthetic eye, because it was considered cosmetic. What was I supposed to do, walk around with no eye? So I prayed every day. Things kept preventing me from getting my procedure done. But I never stopped praying or give up. I kept persevering. I was getting weary. But I never gave up asking God.

This took 8 years to pray through. Finally I got my custom-made eye done. I felt like a freak with one eye, but nobody knew it was a glass eye. Once I was at the eye doctor, and the doctor was checking my eyes with the little flash light. First he did my good eye. Then he did my fake eye. He said, "Tell me when you can see this," and shone the light on my fake eye.

I said to the doctor, "Boy, if I tell you that I can see out of this eye, it would be a real miracle! Because that's not a real eye." The doctor turned all red. He was embarrassed. He knew my right eye was blind, but he had forgotten. Boy we had a good laugh.

In time my left eye has become partially blind. So I am blind in my right eye. And my left eye has partial vision. So now I have only one half of an eye to see with. The doctor won't tell me for sure if that eye will ever go completely blind. This is crazy. I have to take things the way they come and deal with whatever comes my way, one day at a time. I am not alone. I have the Lord and his angels surrounding me, I believe.

The doctors also said that I would be in a wheelchair for the rest of my life. The doctors told my parents that I had very little time left to live, and if I did live I would be a vegetable. Well one day, out of the blue, I began to talk. What a miracle! The staff at the hospital was in awe. I didn't have to have speech therapy.

My parents came to California. They came into my hospital room. Mom handed me a rosary, and said, "Here, pray." Nobody told me what to pray for. My dad looked sad. He looked like he wanted to cry. But I was so happy because the feeling of the Lord's presence was still with me. So I prayed. When it was just me and the Lord. I prayed this prayer with the roseary. That I knew how to do growing up in a catholic church. I was flat on my back. Repeatily saying. Our father who art in heaven hallowed be thy name. Thy kingdom come thy will be done on earth As it is in Heaven. Give us this day our daily bread and forgive us our tresspasses. As we forgive those who tress pass against us. Lead us not into temptation but deliver us from evil. For thine is the kingdom and the power and the glory forever and ever Amen. My dad walked into my room. He came to my bed side. I had the biggest smile on my face. Because of the presence of the Lord.

I said, "Dad, guess what? I have seen the Lord, and He said that I was going to be okay." My dad left the room. It looked like he wanted to cry. My aunt Roxy came in next. She put her chin on my chest and began to cry.

The doctors never could remove the entire bullet. Part of the bullet was stuck in my skull. Doctors said it should not bother me. Because the bullet was lodged in the bone, it probably would not move. Over the years, God has been healing me little by little. As the years pass, I've had many M. R. I. tests done. Each time people in the hospital would just freak out. They could not believe that I was walking around with a bullet in my brain.

I've battled severe headaches of all types, in all forms. For a season I would have them 24-7. This is not good. My last M.R.I. that I had done was the best and last one I will ever need. While I was getting the test done, the radiologist came running over to me. He asked if I had gold inside of my ear. I said no. He was shaken up. He said that some kind of metal was coming out of my ear. The radiologist said that I should never get an M R I done again because this was very dangerous for me with the fragments in my head. I said I have had many done. This did not scare me, in fact I think the radiologist was more frightened than me.

Years have passed. The Lord continues to heal me inside and out. The Lord took most of the bullet out of my skull. There are only a few fragments left. What a wonderful God. The Lord is still healing me. I know he could do it quickly. He chooses to do little by little. The Lord has his reasons. Healing takes time. It's hard to wait.

I suffer from dizzy spells from time to time. Now this is scary. I've been tested once for dizzy spells. The doctors don't know what causes them or how to treat me. I am more afraid of dizzy spells than I am of headaches. The dizzy spells are more dangerous. I can't leave the house if I am having dizzy spells. I could fall down and bang my head hard on the ground, wall or appliances. I couldn't leave my room. At times I would scream because I don't like being dizzy. I don't need to go on rides at the amusement parks. Elevators and escalators were scary for me to go on. My head was all bandaged up. I had no hair only little stubs on my head and they itched.

I began praying with the rosary. I prayed the Lord's Prayer. I kept saying this prayer over and over. Not knowing this is the right way to pray. I prayed morning noon and night. I continued to talk to the Lord. He was my only real friend. Even if i couldn't see him. I knew he was real.

At the hospital, I felt like I was in jail or prison. I had to ask for permission from the doctors to do anything. They seemed over protective. I know they were just doing their job and that they knew best. I had very tiny veins. They would often collapse. Every day for months the lab technicians came to draw blood. They poked two to three times trying to get a good vein, and it hurt. I know they were just doing their job, but I was tired of being poked. I would say leave me alone. I told them they only get to poke me once. Although I was never mean or talked mean to them. They knew I was just kidding around. I couldn't yell at them even if I wanted to. My voice was soft from having all those tubes down my throat. I couldn't yell. I was glad that I could talk though. I know people who have strokes and have to get speech therapy. I was thankful that I could talk.

Eventually because of my collapsing veins the doctors wanted the lab technicians to start using the veins on my feet. Then they decided to give me pills, instead of needles. I was glad. I did not want the technicians poking holes in my feet. I felt like a pin cushion. My arms were all marked from being poked with hospital needles.

I had my birthday in the hospital. I turned twenty-one years old. The nurses and staff pitched in and gave me a beautiful hanging plant for my hospital room. I began to have physical therapy and occupational therapy. It hurt so much to move my legs, arms, and fingers. To make them move was very painful. I never knew that people that had strokes, had to go through so much pain. I never knew how painful a broken bone was. I realized if I wanted to get better, I had to go through therapy. Once, I went to therapy earlier than my scheduled time so that I could get a longer work out. The therapist said if I did too much, I could cause damage. So I waited until it was my time after that. In the meantime I kept on praying and asking God to get me out of the wheelchair.

The Los Angeles judicial court subpoenaed me to come to court to testify against Phil regarding the shooting. The Los Angeles courts wanted me to identify the man who tried to kill my friends and me. The doctors said I couldn't physically go to court. So the court, judge, and jury came to me in the hospital. I did not want to see Phil again. Although I knew I had to do it, it made me physically sick having to see Phil again. I had to make myself strong. I had to do it. My parents were in court as well. I identified that Phil was the man. I also told the court that a dog got treated better than I did.

When we were having court in the hospital, my mom said there was a woman with Phil, and she had a little baby with her. She thought that the baby was Phil's. During court, Phil pretended that he was insane. He pretended that he didn't know who I was. My mom said she wanted to scream and hit Phil.

Phil was convicted of attempted first degree murder with a deadly weapon and was sentenced to a total of eight and a half years in prison for his actions. The first six months Phil served at San Quentin prison, and later transferred to Soledad prison to serve the remainder of the eight years. It was so short. Maybe they should have given Phil a pat on the back and told him to try again, maybe next time he could successfully kill my friends and me. Or anybody else that Phil got mad at. Nobody knew when Phil was going to act crazy again. The woman who kidnapped my baby would have been sentenced to more years than someone trying to commit murder. I think everyone was in shock at the sentencing.

Later, my friend from the club came to see me. She brought me a wig. She also brought a guy friend of hers along. They took Polaroid pictures of us together that day. In the hospital I went to the chapel for church service. I wanted to get out of the wheelchair and receive communion. I was afraid that if I tried to stand up, I might fall on my face. Maybe I didn't have enough faith. I wanted to receive communion. So I received communion. Unity is very powerful. First Corinthians 11:23-24: "Christ's body was broken for us so that we could be made whole."

When I got back to my room after church, there was this program on the television called soul train. Young adults were dancing. I watched for a minute or so. I then felt this pulling for me to get up. I believe it was the Holy Spirit pulling me to get up. I began to get up slowly. Then I stood up. I stood in awe. I began to move as though I was dancing. The nurses were screaming with awe and joy. I could walk a little; they said it was a miracle! Now I was determined, to get out of the wheelchair permanently. So I worked harder than ever before.

I was then transferred to a rehabilitation hospital in Long Beach California where I could finish physical and occupational therapy. I had a long road ahead of me.

Chapter Twelve

HEALING TAKES TIME

In occupational therapy I baked some chocolate chip cookies. Boy they were good.

I called my mom every day on the telephone collect. I needed to hear a familiar voice. My family sent me a picture of my sister's baby girl, in a pink dress. The baby was named Jessica, she was so cute. I had the nurses hang the picture of my niece on my bed railing. I looked at the picture every day, saying to myself that I was going to get better. This gave me motivation and determination to go back to Minnesota to see my niece.

I had an acquaintance Tina that lived in California that was originally from Minnesota. She came to visit me a few times. She was friends with my aunt. Once, while I was in Long Beach, she brought me some Spanish rice. She lived in Pasadena, California, at the time. I had gone to school with this women's sister, Gloria. She lived in Minnesota. She was just an acquaintance. I had grown up with this woman. I went to school with her from kindergarten to twelfth grade. Gloria wrote me once while I was in the hospital, asking me if I had received the Lord as my personal Lord and savior. I wrote back to This woman. In my reply letter to her I wrote I not only had I received the Lord, that I had also seen him in a vision. Apparently, my friend and her friends were praying for me back in Minnesota.

Meanwhile, my son was getting further and further from me. It was hard for the county social services and the foster parents to bring my baby to see me. It was hard for me to accept the fact that California social services wouldn't bring my baby as often as I would have liked to see him.

I met a few people while in the hospital, and we became friends. There was a young lady that had one of her legs amputated. She gave me a gift once, a t-shirt with a picture of tennis shoes on it. It was cute. When I wore the shirt, I thought of her. I wanted to get out of there. Everyone there was in a wheelchair. I kept asking God to get me out of the wheelchair. I believed that I didn't belong in a wheelchair or in that hospital.

The day came when my insurance did not want to pay for me to be hospitalized any longer. I had been hospitalized about six months. This seemed unreal. I was given two options. Either I could go to a nursing home in California, and finish therapy there. Or I could go back to Minnesota and finish occupational and physical therapy there. So I decided to go back to Minnesota. I was getting further and further from my baby. I cried. I wanted my baby to come back to Minnesota with me. It wasn't that easy. Tod was now in the custody of the Los Angeles social services. I wanted my baby. But the truth was I couldn't take care of myself. So how was I supposed to take care of a baby? So I went back to Minnesota without my baby. I felt empty. I felt like I had lost something.

On the airplane ride back to Minnesota, I was embarrassed because I had to ask the stewardesses to help me unbuckle and unzip my pants so that I could use the restroom. I could not use my left hand or fingers.

The occupational therapist made an object for my hand to hang on to, to keep my fingers and hand from crippling and stiffening up. There was elastic around my hand, keeping the object from falling out. I was told if my left hand or fingers stiffened up, they would get crippled up. Then I would not be able to use them permanently. I felt like a freak wearing the object. I could not get myself dressed without help. I couldn't do the simple things such as: tie my shoes, button my shirt and pants, zip a zipper, or snap a button. I suppose I could have tried to do things with only one hand. By the time I undone my pants. I would have gone in my pants. I didn't even try to do it one handed.

Because I felt weak and shakey. It felt strange to go outside and see sunshine and breathe fresh air. I hadn't been outdoors for half a year. This was a very strange feeling. I felt as though I was dead. Or maybe in a deep, deep sleep for many months. And now I finally woke up to a nightmare. That I came back to life, and civilization. In the last months everything was strange and very hard to accept. I had to work very hard to get better and stronger each and every day. Every day was a challenge. I wanted progress fast. Progress was not fast enough for us in the wheelchairs. I met another friend, he had a helmet on his head. He had a plate put in his head. We always talked about when we get out of the wheelchair.

The day came when I had to leave. I said goodbye to everyone. The nurse handed me a black cane to use to walk. I refused to take it. Even though I was a little shaky when I walked, I still wanted to be as normal as possible. I was kind of weak and shaky'

When I got to my parents' house in Minnesota. I was glad to see my family. I thought that when I took off my wig, my brothers and sisters would laugh at me because I didn't have any hair. The thing is when I came back to Minnesota, I came back in style. I was told that was the new look for women to have our hair shaved off. I was amused. My hair started growing back at a fast rate.

I then went to United Hospital as an outpatient, for physical and occupational therapy. The Red Cross would pick me up and transport me to this hospital. Later, they would bring me back home.

I didn't want to believe that my right eye was blind. This was hard to accept. I would cover my left eye and peek through my fingers. Saying yes, I can see. That wasn't the truth. I was given a referral to an eye doctor in Saint Paul, Minnesota. He said that my situation was serious. That my right eye was going to go blind. The truth was it was already blind. I had to accept it. I cried, and told my mom what the eye doctor had said. I thought to myself that doctor was a quack. I believed the eye doctor needed to retire.

I continued to work in physical therapy and occupational therapy. At home my mom had me exercise my left arm and hand. I would wash my mother's hallway stairs every day, exercising my left arm, hand and fingers, so that I could get the left side of my body as strong as I possibly could. The day came when I didn't need to receive therapy any longer. My therapist said my left side was as strong as it could get.

It took about a year for my voice to return to normal. I would frequently reminisce about when the Lord came to me while in California in my hospital room. I still could feel the presence of the Lord. This also made me happy.

My face was numb. My left fingers and hand, still could not totally feel. Sometimes I had a runny nose and couldn't feel it. I could not tell the difference between hot or cold on my hand. I could put my left hand on a stove burner for a brief moment. I could not properly differentiate temperatures. I could not feel my right side of the face as good. When I brushed my teeth, I was doing damage to my gums because I was brushing too hard. The gums holding the teeth in place were slowly diminishing. The dentist always asked if I was using a soft tooth brush. I said yes. In time my teeth hurt. I was afraid to go to the dentist. I thought, maybe I will have to get my teeth pulled out. They hurt. I decided to go to the dentist. He said I needed to use Sensodyne toothpaste. I was relieved that there was nothing serious wrong with my teeth. I did try the toothpaste. It took quite a few brushings to make a difference. It did help. It made a big difference.

Then I was put on medication, to help me to not be paranoid or panic or not have high anxiety. I would walk around the house confused and scared. This medicine made my mouth very dry. I carried water where ever I went. At times I felt sick to my stomach, if my mouth was too dry. In fact, my girls would laugh at me. They said I looked like a freak when my lips stuck to my dry teeth. This was embarrassing, annoying, and humiliating. I had to carry hard candy to suck on. Then they came up with a new toothpaste and mouthwash for dry mouth, called Biotene. So I tried the toothpaste. It did help a little. Now I had to make a choice. To use toothpaste for dry mouth or sensitivity. I then thought I should use the toothpaste for sensitivity, and the mouth wash for dry mouth. My eyes got big when I saw the price for the mouthwash. Everything is so expensive. I always say it's expensive to live, it's expensive to die.

This is a saying I always say. Because it's true. Funerals are so expensive. To live is really very expensive.

I always had good checkups from the dentist. The dentist said I had beautiful teeth. They also said that I was cavity resistant. When I was younger I was afraid to go to the dentist. My mom and dad never took us kids to the dentist. I found out in time that there is nothing to be afraid of.

My schoolmate that I grew up with came to visit me at my mom's house. Our birthdays are only a few days apart. my friend invited me to a Friday night coffee house. The name of the coffee house was called Faith, Hope, and Love Center. There was praise and worship. Then a sermon teaching from the preacher. Sometimes I didn't get home until one o'clock in the morning. I was busy talking, having coffee and snacks. It was stressful on my body as I wasn't physically strong enough to stay up so late. I was still weak from being in the hosital for so many months.

HEALING TAKES TIME

There is no doubt in my mind, that healing
Takes time. You must unwind, keep this in mind.
There is no limit too time. Healing takes time,
it takes time to heal. Especially that, what you
can't feel. You could heal fast, so that the pain
wouldn't last; then it would be in the past.
Healing takes time, so sit back let's make a deal

Rachel Tejeda Morris

It takes time too heal, time never runs out.
So stand up and shout. Don't be in doubt.
Time never runs out; when we get too be with Jesus.
He will be glad to please us. Healing takes time.
I don't ask for much. So stay in touch.

Healing takes time, Have peace of mind.
That in due time, however, healing takes time.
All this will not be a waste of time. You won't
have to hurt as much. Healing takes time,

without a doubt in my mind. This is no shrine
so don't decline now that you have this following
in mind; unwind; meditate, with your mind.
Revealing this to unwind. Go ahead take your
time; healing takes time.

Once my dad asked me why was I coming home so late. Dad said to me, "Don't tell me you were praying all this time." My dad didn't understand about this new found relationship with Jesus. They called it a religion, my family thought of me as some kind of religious freak. I met all these nice Godly people. They were my spiritual family. The pastor's wife gave me a Bible. I had never had a Bible in my life. I began to read the Bible and study some of the parables and scriptures. I began to find out biblical things that I never knew. For instance, I asked the Lord's help to forgive my husband for what he had done to me and my son. I did not know that the Bible said that if we don't forgive others, the Lord won't forgive us.

I was thankful for my new friends. I was excited to go to church and to the Bible studies. Everything was new and exciting. I went to Jesus People church, located in Minneapolis. It was a big church. There were nine different pastors there at the time, and thousands of people. It was humongous. I had never seen such a big church. I had to fight my way to the bathroom. There were so many people.

I went to a Christian camp. I came back talking like a real Christian. There was an alter call for people to get saved. There also was an alter call for people who wanted to be filled with the Holy Spirit, and to speak in tongues. I was excited, I wanted all the Lord had to offer. I went up the wrong line. I did end up getting prayer to be filled with the Holy Spirit, and to be able to speak in tongues. What a blessing to receive lots of gifts from God! In time I learned how the different gifts worked. I was blessed with many, such as faith like a little child. Being an exhorter, which is building people's faith up in the Lord. The gift of prophecy, the word of wisdom, word of knowledge. To be used of God. In time I blossomed, and the Lord increased my gifts so that I could use them within the church. Eventually, I could interpret dreams and visions. I then could interpret the speaking in tongues.

I was simply blessed that God gave me so many beautiful gifts. Let's not forget the fruits of the spirit that we all receive and try to keep using in our daily lives. Galatians 5:22 "The fruit of the spirit is love, joy, peace, patience, kindness, goodness, faithfulness, gentleness and self-control." I began getting blessed by the word of the Lord. The Lord began speaking to me through His word. Each time reading the Bible was different. Even if you read the same thing, it's never the same. It was the most exciting thing I have ever experienced. I no longer needed to get drunk or high from the things of the world. I did experience a feeling of being drunk in the spirit. Sometimes people would say to me they wanted to have what I had. I told them it is the Lord. Yet they could not understand.

I began to see things the way God wanted me to see them. At first when my right eye was blinded, I used to cry frequently. Now the Lord was showing me how blessed I really am. Matthew 5:29-30 says, "If your right eye causes you to stumble, tear it out and throw it away from you. It is better for you to lose one part of your body than for your whole body to be thrown into hell." I got so blessed that my right eye is the one that was blinded and taken away. So what was a tragedy, turned into being a blessing and triumph! I was happier than ever before. I was always smiling. Because i have the joy of the Lord!

My family thought that I was nuts. I was always smiling. When I began to laugh, Oh boy! It was hard to stop. It was contagious. I've seen people laugh and laugh, like they are drunk. I've seen people cry and cry. It's the Lord touching us in a special way. I have experienced both. Also being slain in the spirit. Just falling down from the presence of God touching us. I didn't believe in being slain in the spirit until it happened to me. When I got up from the floor, I was drunk in the spirit. I really did feel drunk. This was unreal, but fun. I loved my relationship with Jesus. I wished my family could experience what I have experienced.

Miraculously, I still felt the presence of God with me. I began to gain a little weight. Just about every night there was some kind of church activity. On Sunday there were two services. On Tuesday there was Bible study. There were only three of us girls. The rest were men.

One night a man hurt his knee. I wanted to go over to him and pray over his knee. I then thought to myself that maybe I should pray for him at my home alone in my prayer closet. I began asking for prayer requests within the fellowship. I would write down and record the day that God answered that prayer request. When I felt down or sad at times, or felt that the Lord was far away, when I looked at the prayer requests I would see that God was here. And yes he is near. Also that he answered prayers.

My son was allowed to come for a ninety day in-home visit. He was flown on an airplane from the state of California. I wasn't sure how I was going to take care of my baby and also meet his needs. My older brother and my two sisters went along with me to pick up Tod from the airport. Tod did not know who I was. He was frightened. I cried because my baby didn't know me.

My mother told me that I should potty train Tod. At times when I disciplined Tod I felt like I didn't want to stop. I knew that this was something wrong like bitterness, resentment even hatred and unforgiveness. I knew that I had to forgive Phil for what he had done to our lives. I asked God to heal me in every way possible. I did not want to hurt my baby. When I saw Tod, I saw his father. This was difficult for me. I called Child Protection Services and told them of my situation. Social Services came and took my baby. I'd rather give him up than to ever hurt him.

Again, this was difficult to be separated from my baby. I couldn't go back in time and fix things. I wished I could. I could never make up to Tod the time we lost together. I couldn't go back and take away all the pain and hurt. For myself I believed I had to keep pressing on to the higher calling that I believe the Lord had for me. I lived in a household of non-believers, my dad and my brothers were often drinking with friends and relatives. Only my mom and one of my sisters didn't engage in alcohol or drugs. Everyone else did.

My grandma was in the hospital. She had severe cancer in her throat. My Grandpa smoked cigars and pipes. Grandma got cancer from second hand smoke. The Lord wanted me to go see my grandma. She was dying. So I took a missionary that spoke Spanish well. She was from Mexico. I had met her through my fellowship. She was a sweet lady. We had the opportunity to pray with my grandma for salvation. Then the Lord took my grandma to heaven a few hours after our visit. I believe this was a divine appointment. It was a miracle. I believe she got to go to heaven after she died, so the timing was right. I was glad that I obeyed the Lord. I was happy because grandma was now in heaven with the Lord.

The Jesus People church, in Minneapolis, was splitting apart. There were a lot of things going on with the pastors and elders. Many people were leaving the church. Almost everyone was going their own ways. The pastor and his family, as well as some of us church members started our own church independently on our own. Other members of the Jesus People church also left, starting their own churches. Jesus People church closed down. It was time for me to move on as well. I was given the opportunity to move into the ministry home with my pastor, his family, another couple, and a few single guys. Also another friend of mine named Cheryl. I was excited to learn. As the ladies were teaching us things, we divided the household chores. We took turns planning, cooking, baking, and all the things in the home. We lived in Turtle Lake, Wisconsin church friend Cheryl eventually got breast cancer. She beat it for eight years. Then it came back and the Lord took her home. Now I believe she's in good hands forever. One day I will see her again.

Chapter Thirteen

THE REUNION

I had a hard time remembering things. This was very stressful for the women in the big house, who also taught me things such as baking, and cooking.

It was a stressful time for me. It was frustrating and annoying; to everyone, not just me. People had to repeat themselves. I am sure that I wore their patience thin. So the pastor's wife suggested that I write on a tablet to help me remember. Things such as directions, recipes, and so on. I began writing these things down to remember. Till this day, I write things down. This helps me remember. For church I take notes. This helps me to remember what the preacher was talking about. Besides this was good spiritual food, for my spirit to remember.

Being forgetful was part of the head injury. When I had something new to learn or a rule at someone's house that I went to, I had to write it down in order to remember.

Then the pastor got some thin booklets from a Christian school his children were currently attending. These booklets helped me with math and other subjects. Common things I needed to know for everyday living. Pastor also taught me how to balance a checkbook, as well as other things, such as shopping for your money's worth.

One day I saw, the pastor's wife spending time with her son playing cars and reading to him. I cried. I never saw such a thing before. This really touched my heart. Now I learned a new way to interact with my own son.

There also was a ministry home for men in our church. That was located in Minneapolis. I began to spiritually grow. We had an omen's Bible study once a month. It was an all-day event. We would have lunch together. It was great.

Meanwhile I kept trying to get a divorce from my husband Phil, who was still in prison at the time. I had to be on a waiting list to get a free lawyer. This took time. For years I waited and waited. The sheriff was not allowed to serve divorce papers in the prison. This took years.

At the same time, I was trying to get my son back. I had to go according to the rules, laws, and regulations of the state and county. I had to get visits with Tod little by little. In time the visits would increase.

My pastor wanted me to see a Christian doctor. I agreed. I still was in need of healing, because of the head injury. I didn't get my menstruation. I had a hard time having a bowel movement. I had bladder problems. I frequently had to urinate. I could not empty my bladder entirely, so I kept running to the bathroom every five minutes. If I were drinking a lot of coffee or water, it was embarrassing if I were at church. I sat up front, so this was a distraction. Most churches didn't complain.

Then I went to a church where it did matter. If we left to go to the bathroom, we could not come back to our original seat. We had to sit in the hallway and listen to the sermon through the intercom. The pastor said that the word of God was important. He said that we should use the bathroom before service. I then trained myself to only having one cup of coffee before church, instead of two. Pastor didn't know that I had bladder problems. He couldn't treat me different than others. So I made myself go before church since I had troubles with my bladder. I could make myself go any time. Then I had to hold it until the service was over. At first this was hard. Then it got easier to do over time.

So I went to see the Christian doctor. I met him when he and his wife came for dinner. We shared a little of what the Lord had done for me. The Doctor and his wife were amazed. The Doctor said to have a bowl of cereal in the morning. So I tried it. I had good results. I had a bowel movement. Then I started to get my menstruation every other month. In time I got it regularly, every month. This was a miracle. This reminded me of when in the Bible Jesus put mud on the blind man's eyes. Then when the blind man washed off the mud he could see. This was awesome.

I began to get severe shooting pains, in my head. I had to take strong pain pills. I've had the shooting pains on and off since my head injury.

I had another visit with Tod. I didn't like being apart from him. I wanted to keep him with me. It wasn't that simple. I had to take my time, and go through the proper procedures and steps. I ran down the stairs. I wanted to cry. I couldn't. So I sat in a chair, feeling sad. Then I opened my Bible. I turned to the scripture, in Psalm 105:4-5: "Look to the Lord and His strength, seek His face always. Remember the wonders, He has done. His miracles, and the judgments, He pronounced."

I experienced another miracle. The pain that was so painful in my head had disappeared. I didn't have to take pain pills any longer. The Lord was speaking to me with this scripture. The Lord was saying, what are you doing crying about what I am going to do? Remember what I already have done. The words just hit me. I was crying about getting my divorce and getting my son back. I needed to remember what the Lord had already done for me. He died for my sins. He saved me. He healed me in so many ways.

The time came when I finally got my divorce. My visits with Tod were going well. He now knew me as mom. The day came when my son could come to reunite with me. Tod was going to be three years old. I made a chocolate cake for him from scratch. Pastor's son and Tod had the same birthday, only the pastor's son was two years older than Tod. They became great playmates. When the boys got into trouble Tod got all the blame. Pastor said I could choose one of the men that lived in the house to help me raise Tod, so I chose pastor because he was the only one in the house that had young children at the time.

We pretended to go bear hunting in the nearby woods. We used tree branches as our guns. Tod wanted to play with a toy gun. I did not want anything to do with guns, whether they were real or not. Pretending that sticks were guns was as much as I could handle.

I would read to my son. Because of the trauma that took place in our lives, Tod could speak better when he was one year old than when he was two years old. So Tod needed speech therapy. I began teaching him how to read. In Sunday school the children learned new scriptures every week. Tod became an excellent reader. I was proud of him. I was glad that Tod had caught up on his reading, and then some.

We lived a few long blocks from Turtle Lake in Wisconsin. Across from us there were several beautiful fenced horses. We walked there every day singing to the horses. The poor horses had to put up with my voice. I am not a singer. Tod did not like to eat his vegetables, especially peas, so he would keep them squished in between his cheeks in his mouth the whole time while walking to the local park at turtle Lake, where there he would spit them out in the sand.

Then the time came when we had to switch houses with the men's ministry home. This was located in South Minneapolis. It was a very bad neighborhood. Once we did switch houses, the pastor seemed to have some peace in his heart. We moved next door to a crack house. You could feel the negativity and overwhelming heaviness there. On our front gate we had the symbol of Jesus. God was preparing me for some kind of change. For now God was my husband and Tod's father.

Tod started Head Start. I loved to participate in the women's get together. The Pastor said that Tod needed help, that Tod needed psychological help. We believed that this was caused from a bad environment. We had to get him out of that particular school. Everyone in the church pitched in for Tod to be able to go to a Christian private school. Tod started to do better.

Tod and I began to draw closer to the Lord. Every night we prayed for a daddy and a sibling for Tod. We prayed this for years. Then I met a man in church. We began to hang out together. We did do a lot of walking.

The time came for Tod and me to move out on our own. God was teaching me and preparing me to live on my own. Tod and I got a duplex of our own. I felt as if I was a little bird that just learned to fly. Now I was on my own. I knew I was not alone. I had the Lord with me and a son to take care of the best I knew how. In our first duplex house together, we lived upstairs. I felt safer to have people below me. It was only a one bedroom, so I let Tod have the bedroom. I slept in the living room, on the couch. We got our first pet cat, we named her Misty. Tod did not have any friends at the time to play with. So he played with the big dog that lived downstairs. When Tod came in from playing outside, Tod smelled like the dog. I would gag and tell Tod to take a bath. It was funny. At times Tod and I played grocery store and sometimes, I would play puppets with him, making Tod laugh.

Tod and I did a lot of walking. Every day we went for a walk, no matter what the weather was like. We walked to see Tod's great grandma Paula, my mother's mother. Great-grandma Paula had prayed for salvation. At times we talked about things in the Bible. Grandma Paula said that some Jehovah's Witnesses came to her house and read the Bible with her.

Having a second chance at life made me so grateful and thankful for everything. I was thankful for my five senses. Even the simple things in life, such as being thankful for the different seasons we have here in Minnesota. Fall, with the beautiful colors of leaves. I was thankful that I could see. In winters not so much for the cold, but the beautiful snow falling from the sky. How at night it looks like little shiny diamonds. To try to catch a snowflake on your tongue. I was thankful that I could taste, although snow doesn't really have a flavor. It still was fun. To hear all the traffic and everything around, I was thankful I could hear. Just listening to the birds sing was beautiful to hear. At times I wondered what the birds were saying. To feel the wind brush through me. I was thankful that I could feel the wind brush my face. My hair flying with the breeze. That

I had feelings, of emotions. In the summer in how the people do their gardens and yards with beautiful flowers and all. I was thankful I could smell the flowers and the fresh green grass being mowed over and over through the summer. Besides the five senses I could walk and talk. Yes I have a lot to be thankful and grateful for.

We would visit with Grandmother Paula. Just about every day we walked a long ways. We didn't mind, we made it fun. We sang and clapped our hands all the way there. While I visited with Grandma Paula, Tod would sit and watch television. Either C.H.I.P.S. Highway Patrol, Hawaii Five-o, Dukes of Hazard or Zorro. I believe God was good to us, taking good care of Tod and I. We were happy and content. Because we have the Lord in our lives. I believe this is the reason we were doing good. Is because of Jesus. That Jesus is number one in our lives.

The first time Tod and I had squash with butter and brown sugar, we thought it was great. We had it again and again. We often went to the farmer's market. We bought a barrel of squash for a good price. We had a little storage room that was kept cool. We stored the squash there so it wouldn't spoil and ate squash every day with brown sugar and butter. We never got sick of it. We also had liver and saute onions.

Tod and I soon met up with a male friend that I knew when we were teenagers. At the time he was Tod's Head Start bus driver. He would sometimes come over to spend time with me and Tod after he was done driving the bus. This man seemed to be lonesome. One late, late night this man came to our home. He was pounding and pounding on our door. I was too scared to answer the door. I pretended that no one was home. He finally left.

We all need Jesus. We all need to forgive. Most important of all we need to forgive ourselves. "So now there is no condemnation for those who belong to Christ Jesus." These are comforting words from God. Romans 8:1 "And I am convinced that nothing could ever separate us from God's love. Neither death nor life, neither angels nor demons, neither our fears for today, nor our worries about tomorrow. Not even the powers of hell can separate us from God's love. No power in the sky above, or in the earth below - indeed nothing in all creation will ever be able to separate us from the love of God that is revealed in Christ Jesus our Lord." This man wanted me to marry him. I said no because we don't love each other. This man said that I could marry him, then he would love me for taking him in to live with me. I believe this man was homeless.

I wanted this man, Tod's bus driver, to be saved. So I went ahead asked him if he knew the Lord as his savior. We once prayed for salvation together. The whole time we were praying, this man was shaking. Later I heard that this same man had committed suicide. He had hung himself.

One Christmas the owners of the duplex gave Tod and I each a gift. Tod received a brown stuffed bear. He named his bear Elizabeth. It was cute. I received a pair of leather gloves. In time the owners of the duplex wanted us to move out. They wanted to move in themselves. So Tod and I had to move. It was hard for us to find a place that we could afford. I eventually found an apartment I could afford on the east side of Saint Paul.

The landlord was not a very nice guy. I believe he stole our food stamps from the mailbox when we first moved there. In those days the county mailed them to your home. Since we lived upstairs of the landlord, I believe he took advantage of the situation and of us. In the winter, the pipes froze. Tod and I had no running water in the kitchen. The landlord would have parties. I could smell the pot they were smoking. There was a crack on the toilet seat. I told the landlord. He said that I had to pay for a whole new toilet. He said that he was calling a plumber. Since this landlord took a very long time to get a plumber, I assumed he was going to have one of his friends act like he was a plumber. This landlord gave me a price in how much I owed him. I knew this guy was trying to rip me off. I knew I had to move. So I called my friend who happened to be a lawyer. He came over and made a list of all the things wrong in my apartment. My friend said that I could sew him. I believed this is not what the Lord would want me to do. As long as this guy didn't try to get money out of me, I would let things go.

I would give Tod haircuts with electric clippers. I got the clippers at a garage sale. I didn't know at the time the type of clippers they really were. I bought clippers that were for dogs. My family was laughing at me and Tod when I showed them the clippers. Everyone busted out laughing.

At times I would be drinking coffee while laughing, spraying coffee all over. Tod got showered with a mouthful of coffee on a few occasions. Some of my family also laughed about Tod riding his tricycle crooked. They laughed so hard. Our tummies were hurting from laughing so much.

Around this time I began going to a technical school for word processing. Secretarial work. I wanted to get a decent job to be able to independently support Tod and myself. I wanted to get out of the county system. I didn't want the government taking care of Tod and me. So I began going to school. One of my friends took care of Tod and the county paid for the daycare.

I continued to go to school. Tod and I kept going for walks and singing and praising the Lord. We walked and walked. We were praising and singing to the Lord. So we enjoyed it very much. We had a great time. Sometimes we saw garage sales, so we would stop and look around. This was turning into an adventure. I did have to stop at a few places to use their bathroom. This was annoying, because sometimes, I had to go into a bar to use their restroom.

I got a nursing aid job. We were all shown how to make the patient's bed. Everyone did their bed very well like a professional. Mine looked like a little toddler made it. The head nurse asked who made this bed? I didn't say anything. I was so ashamed and embarrassed. My left hand and fingers did not do as well as I would have liked them to. This was the side that was paralyzed. So it could not do better. I felt so ashamed and embarrassed to say that I did it. Then I finally said that I made the bed.

I bought a patient hair pieces to do her hair. It was all knotted up and hard to comb. I felt bad for this woman that nobody cared enough to comb her hair. I began asking questions. The staff didn't like the fact that I brought some hair pieces to do this woman's hair. The staff didn't like me asking questions. Later I found out that this nursing home was being investigated. There had been many complaints. Then they let me go. I was very sad that I could not do the things I used to be able to do.

Then I went to school for word processing office work. Through the school I was offered a job. The school even provided a wardrobe for the job. This was great. My first job doing office work, I was very excited. I began training for the switch board. I drank coffee the whole time. While at work, I had to keep running to the bathroom every five minutes. This was not normal. Since my head injury, I could not empty my bladder all the way. I was having trouble seeing where the calls were coming from on the switch board. The staff were talking about getting colored buttons so that I could see where the calls were coming from. I kept running to the bathroom. This did not help my situation. They had to let me go. I was very disappointed and sad. What can I do? Why couldn't I do anything right? I cried. I just wanted to be normal. I wanted to work a job and support my son and myself. I was getting discouraged and my self esteem was beginning to go down. Yet I kept my joy. Because the joy of the Lord is my strength.

THE REUNION

This is the day we pay restitution.
This is the way we will be rejoicing in
Reunion. This is not a resolution of confession.
Yes we have lost a lot of time; however we can't go
back and undo the bad. All we can do is

forget so it won't make us sad;
and we can think of what we are going too have.
This will be on my mind from time
To time. Looking back is it worth a dime?
Would I be wasting my time? Instead of thinking

Rachel Tejeda Morris

what we could have had. We need to focus
on the purpose of believing for what we
can have. One thing is for sure;
whatever happens to us we can endure.
For this I can be sure; I shout for joy!
Now that I have my boy.

MEETING NEW FACES IN DIFFERENT PLACES

If I try not to cry. I would pretend to be a spy.
I would try to take the sty out of my brother's eye.
Yet I have sin somewhere within. So I will keep
my eyes on Jesus until we win; because he is within.
He will keep me close to his heart. Nothing can
keep us apart. For Jesus is in my heart. This is
A precious start. Meeting new faces in different places.

Wait until you hear of all these different
Cases. When you see the look on their faces.
So I will keep my eyes on Jesus. Meeting new
faces in different places. When you walk down
the street watch your feet. Careful who you meet
Be discreet. Be sweet to everyone you meet.
Meeting new faces in different places.

So hold on tight hopefully everything will be all right.
When you see new faces in different places.
You'll' know that everything changes and rearranges.
Changes are good for everyone this has to be done.
This helps us to learn and grow. And get the job done.

You'll be taught the things you should know.
Then you will know which way to go. So you
Must call on the holy one. In order to get things done.
When you see new faces in different places.
Remember it's God's story so give him the glory.
Meeting new faces in different places.

Chapter Fourteen

MEETING NEW FACES IN DIFFERENT PLACES

I was at the grocery store, standing in line. I saw an old friend that I used to work with at a nursing home. Her name is Pauline. She turned white and pale as though she was going to pass out. She said "Em-Em-Em-Ember?" She finally got my name out. I said yes, it's me. She said I thought you were dead. I said nope, I made it. The people in the store were looking at us as though we were crazy. Pauline got a hold of Diane, the girl that I originally went to California with when I ran away with Gene after high school graduation. She came to my apartment with her little boy, Sam. Diane said to me that she knew deep down that I was still alive. She didn't want to believe otherwise.

When she did come to see me, I told her about Jesus and what he has done for me. She was almost afraid of me. I told her that the old Ember was dead and gone. That I was a new creation. 2 Corinthians 5:17 "This means that anyone belonging to Christ has become a new person. The old life is gone. A new life has begun."

I invited her to a Bible study, with Cheryl and Lance. Diane came. I told her about Jesus and she criticized me, saying can you even chew gum?

She was being sarcastic. She wanted everyone to see her son's underwear because she said they were cute. He had Spider-man underwear. Diane was almost afraid of me because I was so different now.

In the meantime, I kept being a prayer warrior. I saw many wonders, works, and miracles of the Lord. I knew that I had to live different. I knew that I had been given a second chance of life to live for a reason. Each day was an adventure. Whatever came my way, I would do whatever was needed. If I could help someone in some way, wherever I went it seemed the Lord would open doors for me. When God opened doors, I walked through them. I knew that I had to respond and be of help or service to whoever crossed my path. I knew that I may never see them again. Each and every day was different than the day before. Once I was the devil's fool. Now I am a fool for Christ.

I never stopped praying for people or miracles. At times I would cry for joy. Because the Lord was answering prayers. The Lord heard little old me. I was amazed that the Lord heard my prayers and actually answered all of my prayers. Even if it was a silly request. When I got up every morning, before I started praying, I would go around the house thanking God for everything I had. I actually went around the house and pointed to everything, thanking the Lord. God must have chuckled at me for repeating myself every day. Yet when I prayed, I also asked every day. So why is it silly to thank God for everything every day? Sometimes, I prayed for many hours at a time. Sometimes, when I wasn't feeling well it would take a lot longer to pray. When I say longer I mean longer. Anywhere from 12-14 hours. Because I would lie down and pray. I would fall asleep a few minutes. Then I would wake up and pray. Sleep, wake up, pray. God is good to be patient with me. In the meantime, I kept asking God to help me in baking, cooking, and everything women should be good in. So when God gave me a husband, and Tod a father, we would be ready. Tod and I never stopped praying for some of these things. Yet I was afraid that the Lord would answer our prayers. Because God's ways are higher than our ways. And when he blesses us. It is over whelming. His ways are better than our ways. So be careful what you ask for. We prayed and waited for many years. We never stopped asking. Besides I always had a prayer list.

This was on my heart, to pray for others every day. I felt like this was my job given from the Lord. I felt like this is one of the reasons why I was alive. Everybody has a purpose here in this world. Everybody has a job to do. I just don't get paid for mine. In the end I will be rewarded. In heaven with the Lord. When there are answers to prayers, this feels like a reward. I guess, you could say this is very rewarding. I felt loved and important to God. I felt like I was doing God's will. I am happy to serve the living God. And to be used for him and his Glory.

God is Love. The Lord only gives good things. Along with love comes peace, contentment, security, a good self-esteem, joy, and laughter. These are things that matter in our life. They cannot be bought. There is no price on these things. The Lord Already paid the price. These things only God can give, the world cannot give. I am so grateful, and thankful. He could have let me die and go to hell. Instead he saved me and is teaching me, each and every day of his ways. God's ways are great.

Sometimes when God answered prayers, it was overwhelming. Because God's ways are higher than our ways, God's timing is different than our timing. We only see in the mirror dimly what God has for us. 1st Corinthians 13:12 "Now I see a poor reflection. Then we shall see face to face. Now I know in part. Then I shall know fully. Even as I am fully known." At times, I would get this burst of excitement come upon me. I would say to the Lord, "What is it God?" I felt something good was about to happen. I am still waiting on the Lord. I trust that He has only good things in store for me. I just have to wait and not be in such a hurry. Because when I am ready for something, the Lord will give it to me. In his time, for the Lord's timing is better than mine.

I never did see Diane or Pauline again. Yet, I keep praying for them, that they would be saved. In time maybe I will see them again in our permanent home, heaven. I have to keep my eyes focused on the Lord. It's the only way that I believe in staying righteous. And to continue to read His word. That is the only way to live.

While I was going to school, I met the counselor of the school. Her name was Darlene. I shared with her what God had done for me. She was amazed. Weeks went by. I didn't see Darlene. Later the people from the school came to me and told me that Darlene was on alcohol and strong prescription drugs. They asked me if I would be willing to help them. I said sure. They said that Darlene always talked about me. The staff said they would like it if I could be there, and that they were going to have a special meeting with the crisis intervention people. So we would know how to approach Darlene. I could not attend the meeting. They called me the next time. They said that Darleen was drunk and high and she had a gun. Darleen was going to kill herself. The staff said could I please come in and help them help her. So I said okay.

I wrote a poem about her name. I put a scripture in it from Proverbs 17:17, "A friend loves at all times." Darleen broke down and cried. At first I didn't want to see a gun as long as I lived. I was scared. I was praying in the spirit. Somehow they got the gun away from her before I got there. We were all relieved.

Darleen had two adult children. They smiled at me and said thanks. They said that I was an angel. I just smiled back at them. Later, we saw Darleen at the vocational, school. She looked like she was going through some withdrawals. She looked terrible. She was pale and shaky. At least Darleen was on the road to recovery. Darleen called me in her office and she said thank you for what you have done for me. She also said that I should become a counselor as well. I said I don't think so. I didn't want to go to college for years. I wanted to do what the Lord wanted me to do. I may never become a movie star. That's quite alright. I am the Lord's star. I have peace, that only the Lord can give. All my life I ran, and ran not knowing what I was searching for. In the end it was peace that only the Lord can give. This is one of my favorite scriptures.

Philippians 4:4-7 "Always be joyful in the Lord. I say it again, rejoice. Let everyone see that you are considerate in all you do. Remember the Lord is coming soon. Don't worry about anything, instead pray about everything. Tell God what you need, and thank him for all He has done. Then you will experience God's peace, which exceeds anything we can understand. His peace will guard your hearts and minds, as you live in Christ Jesus."

One day Tod and I were going for a walk. We heard somebody crying for help. It was an older lady. She could not shut off her water hose. She said that somebody had stolen her glasses. Actually, she had misplaced them. We helped her to calm down. She was extremely skinny. She looked malnourished. We later found out that this lady was an alcoholic. She said that she was afraid of the dark, so she drank herself to sleep. She alienated herself from family and relatives, friends. I took all the food stamps I had and bought her some food. I took the food and put it in a big box then took the bus to this woman's house. I told her that if I had to come and cook for her every day, that I would. She said to me who are you? I just smiled. Then I wrote my name and number down, on her big yellow pages phone book cover that was sitting on a table with her phone. I told her that if she ever needed my help to call me. I prayed for this woman for years every day after. About eight years went by. I continued to pray for this woman daily, not even knowing her name. That was okay. Because the Lord knew her name, and who she was. This poor woman needed help. She needed prayers. So the Lord and I interceded for her. I never gave up. I continued to ask. Until the Lord answered. Finely. For eight years I prayed daily for this woman.

One day I received a phone call from the county. They said they were going to get some help for this woman. They asked me how I knew this woman. I told them that I didn't know her. I just helped her one day to turn off her water. I shouted for joy, after we hung up the phone. I know the Lord is answering prayers.

Next I met a woman who was pregnant. She was thinking of getting an abortion. I told her that was not a good idea. I continued to pray for this woman. When I saw the woman again, she told me that she was keeping the baby and was getting married to the baby's father. I shouted for joy, I was so happy that the Lord had answered my prayer. I shouted for joy!"in the store. I didn't care who heard me. I didn't care what people thought about me. I was so joyfull to not let anybody steal my joy.

I then ran into a woman that I knew when I was younger. Her name is Elsie. I told her what had happened to me. She hugged me and held me in her arms and said that she had a shelter home for abused women and children. Would I be interested working there? At the time I believe I wasn't strong enough to do that kind of work.

My friend then asked me if I would be willing to do a television interview with WCCO television station. I said okay. She said that I could have my face covered so that nobody would see who I was. I said no, that's okay. I'm not afraid. John 4:4 says, "Greater is He in me than he that is in the world."o I went through the interview.

As I walked down the lighted hallway, I saw a woman curled up sitting in a corner. I had to take a second look at this woman. I knew this woman. Her name was Linda. She went to school with my cousin, also named Linda, years ago. She had the same name. She had a lot of hurt, pain, hate, and resentment in her. I wanted to reach out and hug this woman, and tell her that Jesus loved her. My heart went out to her. I did the interview. It never was put on the television. They said that they couldn't get everybody together to do the editing. I knew that wasn't the truth. It was because I talked too much about Jesus. That's okay, it wasn't meant to go on the television. The sad thing is the television station lost my pictures that I lent to them.

Time went by. I knew I was strong enough to work with battered women and children. In the meantime, I kept praying that if God wanted me to work at this omen's shelter home, He would give me a sign. This women was very hard to get in touch with. She was so busy.

The woman's name was Elsie. So I kept praying and trying to get a hold of Elsie. If the Lord wanted me to work with this woman, then He would have this woman call me. Three times in a row I prayed for this. Every time I stopped praying, Elsie would call me. I thought to myself this is no coincidence. Like the story in Judges 6:36-40. This happened three times to Gideon. The test of the fleece. Only the fleece was dry, when all the ground was covered with dew. The same type of thing happened to me three times. I asked God to let this women Elsie call me.

I knew that I was strong enough to work with the women and children. At times I didn't understand why I was running into battered women all the time. In my own backyard, I met up with a woman named Michele. She was very upset because her ex husband was choking her. He was abusive. It seemed wherever I went, I would run into battered women. It was like the Lord was preparing me for something ahead in the future. 2nd Corinthians 1:3- 5: "Praise be to God, and Father of our Lord Jesus Christ. The Father of compassion, The God of all comforts. Who comforts us, in all our troubles So we can comfort those with any troubles. With the comfort we ourselves have received from God. For just as the suffering of Christ, our comforts over flows."

Next I meet an Asian woman, she was very young. She was only a teenager. She had married earlier and had some children. The woman and her family lived in a small one bedroom apartment. That was all they could afford. It wasn't a good neighborhood. The neighborhood had a night strangler going around killing women. There was police, drugs, shootings, and things on our street. I shared with this young woman about Jesus. Later, we prayed for salvation.

I was glad when The Lord opened the door. I felt I could do whatever the Lord wanted me to do. I wasn't afraid. I began working at the shelter home for battered women and children. At first it was hard to see the hurting women and children. What I mean by hurting is the emotional and mental state that they are in when they come for help. Being hurt isn't always physical. I got to share about Jesus to the women and children. Sometimes I got to pray with them for salvation. I did art work with the kids. I didn't need to be afraid. Yes it's sad. All I can do is pray for them. Because this is what they needed at the time.

The Bible says in Mathew 10:28, "Do not fear those who kill the body and are unable to kill the soul. Rather fear him who is able to destroy both soul and body in hell." We were having a fundraiser for the shelter home. We called the event. "Take back the night." We needed somebody to donate food for the event. They said Tom Cruise was going to be the guest speaker. I didn't know who Tom Cruise was at the time. I didn't watch television or movies. At the time I had long hair, it went down to my butt most of the time. I kept it French braided. The women in charge introduced me to Tom, and Tom to me. He was polite as we shook hands. Tom spoke about when he was a kid. He was in gangs. His father was abusive. It was a good turn \out for this event.

Later in time, I was buying a movie for my nephew for Christmas. It was a movie that Tom Cruise was in. When I looked at the cover of the movie, I thought to myself this guy looks familiar. Then I realized that I had met him before. We had worked on an event together. I thought that was neat.

The only other famous person that I can remember meeting is Bill Cosby in the early 70's when the Oz night club opened up. Bill Cosby was a guest. The security guards took a lady and forced her out of the club. I wanted to see if they would chase me away. So I sat next to Bill Cosby. He had a cigar in his hand. He didn't smoke it. He just had it for looks. At the time he was interested in his fans. I asked him if he danced, he said no. If he had said yes I was going to ask him to dance with me. He didn't have a conversation with me or anyone. I got my picture taken with Bill Cosby. Later, when they looked at the picture, they probably wondered who I was. Then I decided to get up and leave. I didn't think that Bill Cosby would be boring.

I didn't realize that God was preparing me for a husband, and a father for Tod All these years praying, not realizing what we were asking the Lord for. I continued to learn the things the Lord wanted me to learn. Around this time, I started to date a man within my church. His name was Bobby. Bobby also liked sugar a lot. At times Bobby became hyper. Then at other times he got loud and obnoxious. For six years I had to hear the same stories everyday over and over.

In those six years I became emotionally and physically sick. My stomach would hurt awful badly, like somebody had punched me in the stomach.

When I told a friend about the many, many, miracles that the Lord gave me, I shared how the Doctor told me to have a bowl of cereal. My friend said, wait, don't tell me. The cereal you ate was' life' cereal. She was being sarcastic. We laughed. Then out of the blue, I didn't feel good. I wanted to cry, because I didn't know what was wrong with me.

I could not get any real answers from the doctors. Nobody knew what was wrong or what caused my problem. At times, I didn't want to go to the doctors. It seemed senseless. I couldn't get diagnosed properly. It wasn't the doctor's fault they didn't know what was wrong with me. After all, I wasn't a normal person. I was very peculiar. The doctor said that it was spasms I was having.

I was scared to go out. I became nervous and anxious about leaving the house. This condition is called agoraphobia, scared to go out in public. I was also partially afraid of having an accident. When I was a teenager I once bled for 8-12 days, plus I got real sick. So I suffered many years. Then I got arthritis in both knees. There were times when I fell down too much. My whole side was badly bruised. The one side of me was all black, blue and green.. I hurt my radar cuff. I had to wear a sling for a while. After a time I had developed arthritis on my radar cuff. I took a test to see what kind of disorder I have, besides PTSD. I found out that I have anxiety disorder.

There are days, when I feel like I am in my 90's, yet people that I knew who were in their 80's and 90's were in better health than myself. I had to remember that I had a tragic trauma happen to me.

That I had been through so much. That I've come so far. That I had accomplished a heck of a lot. So I shouldn't get down on myself, because it could have been a lot worse, like the doctors said. I have to admit that I am glad the Lord proved the doctors wrong.

At times I walked around the house in circles during an anxiety attack. Once I had to catch the bus, and on the way to the bus stop I felt like I had to go number 2. I ran back home. This happened three times. I kept missing the buses. I decided to just stay home. Another time I was trying to go to the pool to hang out. Every time I tried to get to the pool, I felt like I had to go to the bathroom. I kept running back to the apartment. It took so long for me to get to the pool.

At times, I canceled my plans if I was having a hard time. With anxiety and confusion or fear and paranoia.

Bobby always said, "Did I tell you about this time when… ?" We would say yep. Bobby would say well you're going to hear it again. Bobby wanted to get married and have children. I wanted the same as well. With all the medical complications I had, I wasn't sure if I could have any more children. I wanted to find out. So Bobby and I planned our wedding. Most of his family lived out of state. Bobby's father was a real redneck. He refused to come to the wedding. He did not allow Bobby's mother to come to the wedding either. Bobby was the youngest of seven brothers. We would laugh and say seven brides for seven brothers. We would laugh about that movie. Bobby waited seven years to marry me.

I had so much going on in my life that I had to accomplish before I was ready to marry. Bobby knew he was going to marry me. Bobby said he had a dream or vision of me before he met me. Awesome! All of Bobby's brothers and their wives and kids came to the wedding. Our church had just moved to a new rented church building located in Saint Paul on Saratoga Street off of Summit Avenue. Bobby and I were one of the first couples to get married in our new church building. We were sad that Bobby's parents did not come and attend our special day. Yet, we still felt the presence of the Lord with us. We each wrote our own vows to each other. The poem that the Lord gave me was called: "The chosen one."

THE CHOSEN ONE

you are God's son, the chosen one
my man whom I surely can stand.
When you are sick and feel down I will
uplift you, I'll be around. The Lord has

called me to be your help mate. I will give
you the latest update. I will love you, obey
you and build you up. I will see you through

No matter what. Your hands strong and masculine.
Yet you are gentle loving and kind. You have
peace of mind. You have been called to be
my man. A father to my son. Today is the day,
When we become one.
our new life has just begun.

Everything was beginning to fall in place. At first I was discouraged. We could not find enough material for all the bridesmaid's dresses to be done. The women were going to make their own dresses. Finally we got enough so all the women could have the same material. I got my wedding dress hundreds of dollars cheaper than retail price, which was a miracle. I got my veil at a totally different store. It matched my dress perfectly. My wedding veil was hundreds of dollars cheaper as well. I couldn't believe it. At times it was hard to sleep. I was overwhelmed because of all the exciting things that were happening. I kept praying that the Lord's presence would be strong at the wedding. God answered my prayers.

We had beautiful live music. For the reception we had fresh fruit and cake. We couldn't afford much. Bobby's side of the family covered the financial aspects. Everything was so beautiful and dreamy. Afterward we went to a resort for our honey moon, driven by a rented limousine. On my wedding night, it was like I was a virgin again. God made it very special. We had a pillow fight. We took walks around the place where we were staying. We played a Christian game. It was fun. We were only gone for a few days, but it felt like we had been gone a week. God made that special as well. We came back home excited to start our new life together.

Bobby was working nights. We didn't have a car. When Bobby got off of work there were no running buses, so Bobby walked miles and miles. He would tell me about his adventures on the way home. I was worried. Because Bobby would tell me frightening stories. It seemed Bobby always had a black cloud following him where ever he went. Once, a bus ran over Bobby's feet. Then a big huge woman sat on top of him. He said the women took up three bus seats, including Bobby's seat with Bobby in it. Bobby always had stories to tell. Afterward he would laugh about it. But I would worry about him. Especially when Bobby had an incident happen to him daily. Bobby knew that I was a worry wart. At times he gave me more to worry about. Sure we laughed about the stories that he told, yet he knew I would worry. He would say. "I can take care of myself."

We wanted to have a baby right away, so we tried. Even on our honeymoon we tried to make a baby. We had sex so much, yet we couldn't conceive. Sometimes I would clinch my teeth, because I didn't want to be touched.

Bobby couldn't seem to keep a job for very long. He frequently got laid off. We had to go on welfare. We finally got pregnant. We were excited, but I became very ill with morning sickness. I also began to feel like I had to faint. I had to run to the couch and lay down before I passed out. This continued to get worse as the weeks went by. During my whole nine months I was miserable. I kept dreaming about a little baby girl. She was so cute. She had a little pink dress on. She looked like she was only a few months old.

One night a man climbed in our living room window. I happened to get up to use the bathroom, and I saw someone run across the lawn. I thought to myself, I don't see anyone running on our lawn during the day. It was the early hours. I stood and watched for a minute. I didn't know what I was to do. I thought to myself, if I try to wake Bobby up the man might try to hurt us. Bobby had been up all night. Apparently, he had been awake for thirty two hours straight. I don't think I could have gotten him to respond. Then I thought to myself that if I try to hit the man on the head with something, maybe the man wouldn't get knocked out. Maybe then he would try to hurt me. Or even worse kill me and Bobby. I decided to flick on the light. I had my hand on my hip. I said to the man, "What are you doing sir?"

He said, "I am trying to get this guy." The man did not make any sense. Then the man jumped down off the window and ran as fast as he could. When I finally went back to sleep, I had a nightmare, in which the same man was breaking into our apartment. He was sleeping with Bobby and me in our bed with us. That was some strange nightmare.

Chapter Fifteen

WHAT'S YOUR PLEASURE?

It came time to have my baby. There were complications. My baby was going to be a big baby. I couldn't have the baby the normal way. I had to have an emergency C section. My blood pressure shot up very, very high. Something appeared to be wrong with the baby's heart beat. The hospital machines were going crazy. I was going to watch the birth of my baby. After they drugged me up. I started screaming. I yelled put me to sleep. I had gotten a bad reaction from the drug they gave me. Later, when I woke up. Bobby was at my bed side holding our baby. He had the biggest smile. He said "It's a girl."

I looked at the baby. I shouted with joy. I had dreamed of my baby the whole nine months. I said, "This is the little girl I was having dreams of. The whole nine months."

I named her Tammy. One day when I was pregnant and on the bus, I thought to myself, what should I name my baby? The name Tammy popped in my head. I thought to myself, Tammy, yes. That's what I will name her. Tammy Tammy it is. My baby looked like she was three months old. She was big and strong and healthy. I looked like I had been raised from the dead. I looked terrible. My healing time was horrible. I kept getting new roommates in the hospital. I had to wear a catheter I could not urinate on my own. I also had the baby blues. I cried all the time. The recovery time was awful. The doctors gave me a pill. They tried to get me to urinate on my own. I was in the hospital eight days. I still could not urinate on my own.

WHAT'S YOUR PLEASURE?

What's your pleasure? I am with you till
this day's measure is done. In hopes
the battle may be treasured and won.
We have won the victory, we have won.
We have priority we have won.
Remember this gesture you are my pleasure.
When it's time to lecture there is no measure.
That can cause only displeasure. There
is no texture, for you are my forever pleasure.
So I say what is it my dear? What is your
pleasure? I will draw you near, I will
love you forever. This is my treasure...
that you are my pleasure forever and ever.

Eight days later I went home wearing a catheter. I had to measure my urine. They had me self-catheterize. I could not get the hang of it. I had to keep going to the emergency room at the hospital so they could empty my bladder. I didn't want my bladder to burst, I had enough health problems. Finally a nurse came to my house. She showed me how to properly catheterize myself. I still had the baby blues. I cried all the time. I had to be on antibiotics. For the next fourteen years, I had to self-catheterize myself. When I went to a public place I had to stand, and pee like a man, catheterizing myself. Women looked at me like I was a freak. I used to cry all the time, because I felt like I was living in a nightmare. This didn't feel real. Yet it was real and I had to accept all the troubles I was having physically. I also was anemic, so I was exhausted and weak. I looked pale and sick. This is the way I looked after I had Tammy.

I was thankful that my baby was strong and healthy and of course happy. Tammy took all the red blood cells from me. The doctors were afraid of me. They could not believe that I was walking around with no red blood cells. One doctor turned as white as his shirt, he looked like he was about to pass out. Then, he needed a doctor. I decided to not care what anyone thought about me. They did not know how far I had come. Neither did they know what I have been through.

I also had to take oral laxatives and stool softeners on a daily basis to make me have a bowel movement. When I had to go, I couldn't hold it. This was sometimes a disaster. It usually happened when I hadn't gone in so many days. I dreaded the feeling of not being able to be near a bathroom. Once we were at the Mall of America. There was a very long line. I had to relieve myself of number one and number two badly. I cut in the front of the line and told the ladies I was sorry. I said I could not hold it. Another time I was at a fast food place and there was a long line in the women's bathroom. I couldn't hold it so I went in the men's bath room. The coast was clear. This was upsetting. I did not want to go out. I knew that I couldn't hibernate forever. Once I was on the city bus. I had to go bad. I couldn't wait until I got home. This was embarrassing and humiliating. Oh I lost it. It seemed to me that the bus driver started to cough and gag when I walked by him. I am sure this was very unpleasant to smell.

I then had to wear Depends diapers for adults for precautions. Now the only depend I use is I only depend on the Lord. Once we were taking Tammy for a walk in the stroller. We saw some friends of ours. I happened to have an accident. My friend smelled it and said poor baby needs their diaper changed. He didn't know that the poor baby was me.

For fourteen years I was on antibiotics. I prayed every day that I would not get an infection. Either a bladder infection or a urinary tract infection. God did answer my prayers. In the whole fourteen years I had to catheterize myself, I only got two infections. One bladder infection, one urinary tract infection. What a miracle. Now I don't have to catheterize myself any longer. It's taken many years to heal. God is still working in me. Spiritually, mentally, emotionally and physically.

Bobby decided to adopt Tod. They both went to the library and picked out Tod's first, middle and last name. They seemed to come up with something they both liked. Shortly after, Bobby was working a newspaper route company. We still did not have a car. Bobby's older brother helped us get into a little house as well as purchase a brown colored station wagon for Bobby to drive.

Bobby was working two or three jobs. Bobby was getting more and more emotionally burnt out. It seemed as though Bobby was going to have a nervous breakdown. He began losing his temper at times, yelling and screaming. He made Tod go with him on the newspaper route. Early each morning and in the dead of winter they would both walk in the early cold delivering newspapers to various customers. Tod was only a little kid at the time. Once in the dead of winter while they both were delivering newspapers, Bobby apparently lost his temper with Tod. Bobby claimed he was slowing him down.

So Bobby slapped Tod and knocked Tod down in the snow bank. Another time we were at a bus stop and Bobby got upset with Tod. He told Tod that he was going to slap him. A women was there. She said she would call the police on Bobby. We did have good times as well. We did do a lot of baking. Once Tod put too much sugar in his cereal. Bobby made tod eat it all. Then he made Tod sit still. Poor Tod he had the shakes. Trying to keep still. Bobby laughed about it. Then Tod punched his calculator. And cracked the screen with his fists. He told Bobby that he pushed the buttons ever so lightly. Bobby laughed. He thought that it was funny. Sometimes I got the giggles at the wrong time. Bobby got angry, like at times when we were trying to pray together. We would hold hands and pray. I began to laugh. And also when I got to tried. It's like I was drunk. I couldn't stop laughing. I think it is better than being crabby and crumpy. I was not doing very well emotionally, mentally, physically at the time. For a long time. At church I would cry. Nobody ever said a thing, so I didn't say anything either. I was sad all the time. I would act happy around my girls, because they made me happy. I didn't want them to know I was sad. I wanted to commit suicide at times.

For our third wedding anniversary we had a romantic dinner. Bobby had a limo pick us up drive us around town for a few hours. When we got home we had a romantic evening. I conceived my third child. I became very sick again. Bobby was not happy about the news, because I had a bad pregnancy with Tammy and because we were struggling financially. I was scared to death to have this baby. I was very sick. When Bobby told his brother that I was pregnant, his brother said that we were digging ourselves into a hole. I did have two flase labors. Maybe I was anxious to get the birth of my baby over with. I was scared to go through another laybour. I was afraid I was going to have a hard time and that it would take too long. I was anxious to get this birth of my baby over with. I was afraid that I wouldn't remmber how to breathe.

I couldn't wait until the birth of this baby was over. Because I was scared to have the baby, I went into labor early. The baby was breech, the feet where coming out instead of the baby's head. This was not good. The doctor wanted me to have a c section. Instead they decided to turn the baby. This was a very painful process to go through. It was horrible. They took these long forceps that were sliver like sliver ware. They were huge. They looked like gigantic tongs that we cook with when we deep fry foods. This was not deep frying. This was for real, my baby was well done and ready to come out into this world. No matter what position she was in. She wanted out.

They did manage to turn the baby so the head was coming down instead of the baby's feet. I never wanted to have another baby after this. Bobby finally agreed that I could have my tubes cut and tied. Bobby wouldn't let me get it done after I had Tammy. I had my second girl.

She was three weeks early. She was seven pounds. Just the right weight. I named her Cassie. It was good for Tammy to have a playmate to grow up with. Tod liked rocking Cassie in the rocking chair. Tod seemed glad that God answered our prayers. We asked the Lord for a baby, and God gave us two babies.

Tod loved having a baby sibling. Tod had anger and jealousy in his heart, which is understandable considering some of the abuse he went through. Tod had a hard time with other schoolmates as well as some local neighborhood kids. They made it hard for Tod to play sports, or anything of that nature.

Tod became very difficult to deal with. Tod was playing with the furnace. He could have blown the house up, with us in it. Bobby and I decided to place him in a county foster home where there he would have more structure. Tod was placed into a permanent shelter foster home in Saint Paul with a woman. Tod was sexually, physically, and mentally abused in her care for the next year and several months thereafter. Tod's behavior got worse from the abuse. Social services and children protective services removed Tod from this home. Due to over-excessive abuse from within this licensed county facility. Tod was then placed at another foster home in Saint Paul with an African-American family. Shortly after, Tod was put on multiple psychiatric medications for alleged depression. I believe some of the types of medications Tod was prescribed over the years. various doctors and so called professionals impaired and damaged Tod emotionally, mentality and physically.

Tod then got placed into a treatment center for troubled boys in Minnesota. Tod's social worker was a Caucasian tall, skinny man. He had white hair that was thinning on the top and often rode a motorcycle to and from work. Tod looked up to and respected this man. Tod and others were physically abused by some of the staff. This treatment facility also had Tod on numerous medications that I doubt he benefited from. At the time, it was as if he was treated as an experimental lab rat.

Shortly after his release from a seven to eight month lengthy stay at this place Tod was returned to his original Saint Paul foster home. Tod was re-enrolled at the facility for ongoing counseling and psychiatric treatment in addition to being placed on various different medications throughout his younger adolescent years.

Over the next several years Tod was placed in a boy's facilityThis was located in Ham Lake, Minnesota. Some of the children and minor adolescent placements placed there with him were allowed to smoke cigarettes on a daily basis they received from facility staff. Some staff, one much older female in particular, smoked packs of Lucky Strikes. She often gave Tod cigarettes. I believe Tod was racially mistreated and physically abused at this boy's affiliates.

Tod was placed on juvenile probation within Anoka County for an extended amount of time due to a racial conflict with a younger male that Tod had gone to school with in Anoka County. It appeared only Tod was disciplined, not the other young man. Within a few years' time Tod was placed in several different facilities, homes and shelter placements around the Minnesota area. He was placed at another facility in Saint Paul where the children there were also allowed to smoke on the premises. He was also sent briefly to Saint Paul to another facility, for boys for a short time period where he was physically threatened by older placements.

Tod began to run away from some of these placements. He was laughed at, mentally abused, and picked on by older boys and placements. Tod was also sent into another treatment center located in Willmar, Minnesota. There he was again placed on numerous medications for alleged depression. It seemed Tod kept going in circles. Partially due to the medications and partially his living circumstances. Tod would do well for a little bit. Then he would go backwards. Tod was placed in a Wisconsin-Minnesota foster home where the woman was divorced. She had other teenagers living at her home as well. She used Tod as if he were a sex doll or toy. She also had Tod do all the cleaning, cooking and baking, for the household. Tod was being used for this woman's pleasure. This woman had done similar sexual things with another teenage boy around his age. I can't believe that this women kept her license for fostering children. She is an abuser. I don't understand. This is crazy.

Bobby once had a motorized moped. Bobby blamed Tod for putting water in his gas tank. The engine blew out. Bobby could not use it anymore. Bobby frequently blamed Tod for things. Once in the basement, I interrupted Bobby while he was smashing a wooden cribbage paddle on Tod's naked butt. I heard Tod screaming, and I ran downstairs to the basement. With a broom in my hand, I started hitting Bobby with the broom. I thought Bobby was out of control. It was the only way at the time that I could stop Bobby from hitting Tod.

Kids at school often teased and gave Tod a hard time. Tod went into the hospital several times while on various different medications for attempted suicide and depression issues. Tod's stays in the hospital were not all too pleasant at times. Somehow Tod fell out of the second floor window at the hospital in Saint Paul, gaining a mild concussion. He broke out of the children's locked unit through an old Plexiglas bedroom window. At the time he was under the influence of medication such as Risperdal. He had to wear a neck brace for weeks.

Tod kept moving from one placement to the next. Getting the right help and living placement was difficult. Meanwhile, Tod was being drugged with many kinds of unnecessary medications and little control over the matter or situation. Meanwhile the doctors were trying to find the right kind of psychotropic medications. I felt as if I couldn't protect Tod from Bobby hurting him. I couldn't keep the foster or placement people from hurting Tod either. My hands were tied. Tod was stuck in the system.

I never wrote Tod or called him. I never sent him cards for birthdays or holidays at the time. I had my hands full. Besides I was suicidal myself. It was as if I blocked that time frame from my mind. Maybe part of it was that I didn't want to remember that chapter of my life. It's like I wanted it erased from my mind. I was in my own troubled state of mind. I couldn't see beyond my own little box of space. It seemed to me as if the girls were twins. Being close in age. Now this was very challenging.

Bobby continued to work two or three jobs just to make ends meet. Bobby verbally threatened to have me put away. He also threatened me that he would take the girls away from me. At times I felt depressed and suicidal. I laid in my bed watching the girls make a mess of the house. When I was cold I would put a sweater on then I would put one on Tammy. When I got warm I took off my sweater. Then I would take Tammy's sweater off. That's probably how she got the idea that she had to change ten times a day. You could not walk in the girl's bedroom without stepping on clothes or toys. Their room was a disaster.

I began to have sharp pains in my stomach. I went to the doctor. I found out I needed a gallbladder operation. I had to get the operation. I had no help. It was the Fourth of July weekend when I had the gall bladder operation done. I got a gigantic scar on my tummy. A few weeks later they came out with a new technique where they only made two little holes in the belly button. You couldn't even tell that you had surgery. Wouldn't you know? It had to happen after I got my gall bladder out. The doctor gave me permission to get wheeled to the top of the roof so that I could watch the fireworks from the state capital. I didn't feel good enough to even look outside my bedroom window where I could see the fireworks. I was scared to go home. I didn't know how I could take care of the girls. They were a handful.

Tammy loved to climb. Cassie loved to try to get things that were hard for her to get, even if it took her all day. The girls wrote on the dining room wall with crayons. Bobby laughed and said that it was nice art work. Bobby got a few parking tickets. The girls got a hold of them. So Bobby missed his court date. When he went to the court to pay his tickets, one officer was getting off duty while the other one was coming on duty. Bobby was placed in a holding tank. Then was placed in a different holding tank. bobby was witnessing to the other prisoners. The judge asked why Bobby was in jail. Bobby said that he was in jail for traffic tickets. The judge said, "That's ridiculous." I thought to myself. This could only happen to Bobby. Once I was busy doing laundry. I didn't even notice that Tammy had left the house. It was raining outside. Tammy walked 3 blocks away. She managed to cross the street safely. She was playing in the street sitting on the curb. In the rain. In front of a bakery. Tammy happened to have a book of mine with my name. The bakery got a hold of me. Tammy always takes off on me somewhere. And I cant find her. This is hard on my heart. I think Tammy wants me to die young of a heart attack. I bet the people at the bakery were thinking that I am not a good mother if I didn't notice that my baby was gone.

Another time Tammy was going to follow a guy that came to our apartment complex. He was dating a women who lived there. I was glad I saw her trying to follow the man on her bike. I would spend lots of times crying because I couldn't find Tammy. Once she was in somebody's garage with two drunk guys and a lady. The women was not drinking. I was glad my baby was safe. Once when we went to the Mall of America, Tammy took off again. We had the security people looking for her. Once at church Tammy went in the back of somebody's truck and fell asleep. I was crying. Nobody was taking it seriously except me. People started to help me find my baby. She must have been three or four years old. Then somebody found her sleeping in somebody's truck. Good thing they didn't leave out of town.

We had a custom made rocking horse that I had when Tammy was younger. Cassie was just crawling. Her biggest ambition was to get on that rocking horse and ride it. Every day she tried. Finally she made it on top of the horse. She didn't get to ride it, she fell over. Oh well, better luck next time. Cassie eventually got up on the rocking horse. She learned how to ride it herself. Cassie loved to learn. She enjoyed watching Sesame Street. Tammy was good at observing things or noticing things other people didn't. She was excellent at finding things. Whenever we could not find something we'd ask her to find it. She always found what we were looking for.

A social worker from the hospital came to see me after my gallbladder surgery. I told her my concerns, that I was afraid to go home. I told her that I didn't know how I was going to take care of the girls. So the people in the hospital helped me get things arranged for me to go home. I was to have a PCA to help me with the girls while Bobby was at work.

Bobby became abusive. He would yell and scream. I once bought him a tie rack to hang his ties up. Bobby yelled, and screamed at me up and down. Then turned around and hung the rack up. So I got him an old fashion VHS movie "Charlie Chaplin." He yelled and screamed at me. Then turned around watched the movie and laughed and laughed. He once took the Sunday newspaper rolled up. The paper was thick. He hit me on my side of my arm that was paralyzed out of anger. The Sunday paper used to be thicker than it is now days. Also the things we buy now the prices went up and the quantity went down. Another time Bobby wouldn't let me go to the bathroom. He was yelling and screaming at me. He swung the door open so hard I flew into the tub. I was hanging on the side of the tub.

Although we did also have some good times. We did do a lot of laughing together. You had to have a sense of humor. I always said that when the Lord disciplines the angels, the Lord would tell the angels that they had to take care of me. We'd say the angels would shake and say no Lord, please not her.

We had a dog named Tanner. When I was mad, he was mad. When I was sad, he was sad. If I was happy, Tanner was happy. One day I was mad at Tod So Tanner got mad at Tod. Tanner jumped up and bit a hole in Tod's shirt. We laughed about it. Bobby was very mean to Tanner. He made poor Tanner nervous and scared, which made Tanner urinate onto the floor.

Once we invited some friends over for dinner. We had a turkey dinner. We had everything ready. Tanner decided that he was going to test the food for us. Tanner took the whole tray of turkey and knocked it on the floor. The couple we had over for dinner came on time. So we all sat down to eat. As we were eating, Bobby says to our guest, "I hope you don't mind eating the meat after it had been on the floor. Sorry the dog took the whole thing and knocked it on the floor. He decided to have a feast." The couple already had the meat in their mouths. You should have seen the look on their faces. You know we never had them over for dinner again. In fact we are not friends any more. We don't talk to each other. We lost touch with them. And them with us.

In fact the last time we saw them was at their wedding. Bobby and I were late. I had knee high nylons and the elastic was not too good. My nylons fell down to my ankles. This was very embarrassing. I wondered why the guys greeting people at the door were trying to hold back their laughter. I looked down and saw my knee high nylons had turned into ankle high nylons. We were late for the wedding because Bobby and I were arguing. So we missed the wedding. Then I show up with ankle nylons. I bet these people had fun laughing at us.

Bobby began to argue with the nurse assistant about being black in America. Bobby was Caucasian, how would he know. The nurse assistant was black.

We did have some good times together. Bobby would take Tod and me for long bike trips. Bobby acted like we were in the army. Bobby was the drill sergeant. Bobby was hard on Tod and me. We did travel all over on our bikes. Taylor Falls, Little Canada, William O' Brian state park, Stillwater, Edina and the Minnesota Zoo in Apple Valley. At times we would take turns giving Tammy and Cassie a ride in the baby buggy. Tod and Bobby were the main ones carrying the girls on the back of their bikes. I carried some light supplies. We biked places you could go in the car. Sometimes it was too hot. We still went biking. When we took a break we would have a light snack. Then the girls got to play at the park of whatever town or city we were in at the time. No matter how hot it was, Bobby made us go. Once it was a hundred degrees. When we went down the hill, the wind was like flames of fire hitting our face. It was so hot. Another time we were in a town when it started raining. I lost control of my bike. I flew off my bike. I hit the cement street so hard. Good thing I was wearing a helmet. I don't think I could survive another head injury. God was looking out for me again. Again the Lord protected me from the world trying to destroy, and kill me. I am so glad that the Lord is on my side. That's good that the Lord fights my battles for me.

BE BOLD

You must be bold you have been
told. You are being molded.
Don't worry you won't be scolded.
You have been bought for a price.
You ought to know that's nice.

The day is coming when you will be
in paradise I won't have to tell you twice.
You must be bold you have been told.
Before you're old. I will keep you in
my hands to have and to hold.

This is how the story is told.
If you are near to my heart.
Nothing can keep us apart.
If you unfold the secrets of my heart.
Be bold you have been told.

Chapter Sixteen

BE BOLD

I did a lot of crying. I was not in a good state of mind at the time. There was no sense saying anything to anybody. I had to keep things to myself. I had to be strong for the girls and myself. I had to be bold.

Bobby stayed up all night saying that his back hurt him. Every time he went to the doctor, the doctor said there was nothing wrong with his back. This went on for a while. Bobby wasn't doing well. He tried to hurt himself. So Bobby went into the hositail for a while. Bobby wanted me to go to a group with other people that had a head injury. I rea lly didn't want to. Because they could not handle what I had to say. Strange Bobby wanted me go to some group that got together that had head injures. I went once. My story was too much for them. I could help them. They couldn't help me. This is how it was every time I tried to get help. So basically I gave up trying to get help. I had to help myself. With the Lord of course. I couldn't do anything if God was not in it. It's only because of the Lord, that I can do anything. Bobby ended up in the hospital. Bobby said that he had thoughts that were not good. That he wasn't safe to be around. So Bobby had to move out so that the girls and I would remain safe. I was scared to live by myself with two little girls. I did do a lot of crying. I must have been in deep depression. I must have looked real sad from crying so much. Because everywhere I went. People would ask me if I was ok. They would say are you alright Ma'am? This went on for a while. I had just started to see a therapist. I told her what was going on. Then I kept crying. I couldn't stop. My therapist felt bad for me. She didn't know how to *contort* me. I did stop seeing her. It seems when ever I get some professional help, I only see them for just a while. It seems that the person could not handle my story. So it was just the Lord and me again. It was alway's the Lord and me.

Bobby ended up in the hospital. The doctors put Bobby on too much medication. This hurt Bobby in the long run, because Bobby began talking verey strange after being over-medicated. Bobby never talked the same or walked the same. At times he fell down. In time, Bobby and his brother sued the doctors for over Bobby. All the money in the world is not going to make Bobby any better. Bobby needed a miracle of healing.

At home I couldn't get enough of the Bible. It was like some type of healing that was taken place. With in me.

Tammy went through something called regression, where she went back in years in her mind. We would go to the grocery store, and Tammy would start crawling on the floor talking like a baby. I took her to get professional help. It was hard to find good help, help that you could trust. Tammy needed healing. The doctors were tying to find some answers. Tammy would have bad nightmares. She wanted me to stay up all night with her. The doctor gave me something to help me sleep better. My brain and body needed to go in a deep sleep. Because I had constant aches and pains. This diagnosis is called fibromyalgia. I had to diagnos myself. A friend of mine called me and told me that a woman was on Tv talking about this illness. I told my Doctor. At first my Doctor did not agree. Then soon after my Doctor agreed. That I had this disease

We lived only a few blocks from a bar in Highland Park, Minnesota. Sometimes, people would walk down the street from the bar. They would be very loud. Then once I heard a lady outside asking anyone for help. I was too scared to go see what was going on. I stayed in my apartment and listened to all the commotion. The next day, I found out that it was a woman locked out of her apartment that lived in the building. We lived in a nice neighborhood. A few blocks away it was ghetto. They had shoot outs and SWAT team there. A gas station got robbed. A man was shot. Crime was everywhere.

One time in the middle of the night somebody tried to break into the girl's bedroom. I was too scared to move. So I prayed. Something good happened for the girls and me, because whoever was breaking in got scared and ran away. I was holding my breath as I prayed. I know it was the Lord watching over the girls and me.

We were trying to get our lives together. I had to be bold for all three of us. Tammy needed therapy that the doctors recommended. I took her to a female therapist. This therapist would frequently call in sick. We drove to a canceled appointment many times, not knowing it was canceled at the time. Just a general waste of our time and gas. We had to get somebody else.

Cassie on the other hand was having severe leg cramps and pain, which made it hard for her to walk. I kept taking her to the doctors. Nobody could diagnose Cassie. Nobody had answers. This was very hard on us all. We kept going to the doctors to try and find out what was wrong. This was very exhausting, going to appointments for both girls. I did not drive, so I had to call for transportation. Sometimes we had to wait a long while. In the winter, it got dark early. This made us even more tired.

The doctors eventually wanted Cassie to get therapy as well. I took her a few times. Both girls were going to the same place for therapy. The specialists there decided Cassie did not need therapy after all, just Tammy. Tammy missed out on things which took place at school. They had a live penguin, once. Tammy missed out. Doctors could not find out what was wrong with Cassie. The Doctors came to a conclusion, that it was linked to stress. Cassie also had frequent sinus infections, all the time.

I kept praying to the Lord. I asked what I should do about divorce. The Lord gave me a scripture from second Peter 2:22, "It is happened unto him, according to the true proverb, a dog has turned to his own vomit again. The pig that was washed to her wallowing in the mud." The Lord was showing me that Bobby would hurt us again. I needed to get out of this marriage. I knew that God hates divorce. Yet in circumstances such as ours, the safety of my children and myself seemed most important at the time. In time we all got better emotionally, physically, mentally and spiritually. The girls and I began to pick up the pieces of our lives. We had to move on.

In the meantime, I had to see a therapist, because of my nonstop crying and depression. While I was seeing her, I began to have flash backs of events that took place in my life. I thought that maybe it was only a dream or nightmare. Then I had to stop denying that it was real and that this happened to me. I began to cry and told my therapist that I was molested as a child. I couldn't believe that I had pushed it away from me so far as to believe it didn't happen to me. That it was only a dream. Or in this case, a nightmare. In order to receive healing, I had to admit that this did happen to me and to stop denying and pretending that this never happened. Then healing can began.

The girls and I began to receive showers of blessings. We got a membership to the Jewish community center, which we lived across the street from. It is like a Y M C A. We got a real steal of a deal. I began to pay all the bills that Bobby left me stuck with. Bobby was not paying any bills at that time. I'm not sure what he did with the money.

Bobby always talked about saving money. Bobby always talked about going to the woods. Living for free, no running water, no electricity. I did not like when he talked about it all the time. It made me nervous. I then began to have anxiety. From Bobby talking like this. Bobby also began to buy me dressess. I wondered why Then in time Bobby to told me that he was going to retire early. That i could get a job and suport the family. This had to be a joke. Because i was not healthy enough to work outside of the home. I had too many health issues. This still made me nervous. And made me scared.

When he talked like that. In the mean time I had to work on my own fears. I had to overcome obstacles in my life. We had an outdoor pool. It took me seven years to swim to the deep end of the pool after the incident in California of almost drowning. I never wanted to swim again. I knew that wasn't going to be possible with two little girls that loved the water. Both girls learned how to swim at a very early age. When Cassie was two, I put a life jacket on her. She learned on her own. Tammy was about three or four years old. They both were excellent swimmers. I would pack us a lunch and snack, and we would stay down at the pool all day during the summer when the kids didn't have school.

Once there was a man in our pool, we didn't know who he was. He was dead. The caretaker jumped in the water and tried to revive him. It was too late. The dead man must have been a guest of someone living in our apartment complex. The dead man had a scar by his heart, like he had heart surgery. Everyone was freaked. We all were scared to go back into the pool. Then things went back to normal. After a few hours. Meanwhile I have to work on my fears. We never did find out whose guest this was or who the man was.

I almost drowned a few times in the pool. At times I would get flash backs, of when I almost drowned in the ocean, in California. Then I panicked. Then I would start drowning. Another time a kid jumped into the pool. He hit me hard on the side of my head and ear by accident. My head and ear hurt for a while. It felt like I got hit with a brick. I panicked, and started to drown. A man was in the pool, he asked me if I needed help. So the man held out his hand to help me. I stepped on the man's head as if he was a ladder. I was drowning the man. We both managed to get out of the pool. Another time my son and I were swimming on our backs. Tod pulled my arm down into the pool. I panicked. I started drowning. Tod tried to help me. Of course I panicked and started to use Tod like he was a ladder. I stepped on his head, and I was drowning him. We both managed to get out of the pool. We were the only people at the pool at the time.

I keep on working on my fears. I would call Tammy Tammy the tadpole, and Cassie cassie the mermaid. At the Jewish Community Center pool the girls embarrassed me. They would say, "Mom, it's not that deep. Come on mom."

We went to camp each year with the church. That was our vacation. It was great in the lake. A little girl said to me, "Don't be afraid, Jesus is with you." I know that was a word from the Lord. God can and will use kids to minster to you. At times I may have panicked.

Bobby always talked about saving water. He would only take sponge baths. Bobby also called me Mom. The house that we had lived in became a shambles. Bobby tried to put new cabinets up in the kitchen. I had to wash dishes in the bath tub for months. Bobby tried to remodel the basement. Then it got flooded. That was not Bobby's fault. There was also a small crack on the front stair of the house. He tore them all apart with a sledge hammer, saying he was going to get new stairs. Now we didn't have any stairs in the front of the house.

I called 911 at least twice a week. It was hard for me to take care of two little girls by myself. Tammy was climbing up a rocking chair, and she got her leg stuck. She kept putting her arms out for me to pick her up. I couldn't, and she did not understand that I couldn't pick her up. She cried. I didn't know what to do. So I called 911, and they came all right. The police came escorting the ambulance and firemen. They took liquid dish soap, and greased her leg so that they could slide her leg out. I bet these guys had a good time laughing at me and my girls and the predicaments we got into.

Bobby broke the garage door so we couldn't use the garage anymore. Bobby had backed up the car and hit the door, accidentally. Next Bobby wanted to make a shelter for his car. Bobby also wanted to make an emergency way out of the house in case there was a fire. All these projects were being done at once. There were big holes in the ground outside from Bobby digging in the dirt. The kids could have fallen down in the holes and broken or sprained their ankle or another part of their body. We would not have even known they were down there.

I remember Tod had picked some dead dandelions for me and he gave them to me. Once he earned some money shoveling snow around the neighborhood. He earned enough money to buy me a special gift at a nearby neighborhood thrift store. Tod purchased me a beautiful, antique jewelry box. He was my first born. My special one. My only son. I can never make up for lost time. I can only focus on now and live for today, making each and every day good.

We never stop learning. There's always room for improvement. We have a great teacher, the Lord.

One day I got angry at the kids because they were dropping food onto the carpet. I began ripping the carpet up. It took me eight hours to do while Bobby was gone. I was so exhausted. I was pregnant with Cassie at the time. Bobby just about flew through the wall when he got home. Because there was no carpeting on the floor, it gave Bobby quite the surprise when he opened the front door. The bare floor was not too pretty to look at. I felt bad that I had done that later. I had no money for a vacuum cleaner. So I had to sweep the carpet extra hard with a hand broom.

At times Bobby was destructive and clumsy. He broke and ruined many things in the house. He would say, "I'll buy you another one."

He said he would get me a new one of whatever he broke. That was just a joke. He never replaced what he broke. It seems that Tammy had the same habit. She would also break things.

Winter had come and gone. Still there were big holes in the yard. Nothing was finished, only half-done jobs. That was the first house I have ever had in my life. I don't know if I would ever have another house. In the end we lost the house. We also lost our dog, Tanner. We lost our car. The engine blew up. Bobby didn't put oil in it. We all needed total healing, in every aspect of our lives.

RIGHT IS RIGHT

I have been with you before there was time.
I know this without a doubt in my mind.

Rachel Tejeda Morris

You belong to me and I will not let you go.
Just take your time go with the flow.
Don't be in such a hurry, you don' have
to worry. Everything has a time and a purpose.

People may say you are peculiar, that's quit
all right. Put up a fight Hang on tight.
Right is Right. Wrong is strong. Do not
prolong. Be strong now come along.
Do not prolong the song that I long
to sing to you my dear. Do not fear

be of good cheer my dear. I am near
my dear. be gentle and sweet I know
how to handle the petite. Be discreet
please be neat. It won't be long.
You'll come along singing a song.

So come along, right is Right wrong is
strong not for long. Now that's out
of sight. Right is right Hang on tight
everything will be all right.

Chapter Seventeen

RIGHT IS RIGHT

The girls began taking steps towards positive healing. Healing relationships as well as healing family loss. Currently, their dad was gone. Their big brother was also gone. We also had lost our home. We lost our car. In the meantime we kept going to church. We kept praying to the Lord. We believed that everything was going to be okay anyway.

The girls and I moved to a new apartment. We wanted to start fresh. meantime Bobby kept calling and calling. Finally I told him that I was going to get a divorce and that we did not want contact with him. Bobby agreed. I had to do what was right for the girls, and myself. While we were getting on with our lives, we had to go forward instead of letting things get us down.

Many years went by. I got in touch with Bobby. I wanted to find out about the family's history. Tammy had her days and nights confused. The doctor was trying to find the right medication and the right dose. Tammy had followed the path that Tod did. To get help, Tammy went into a year-long treatment facility where she could learn skills in how to deal with the mood swings. Tammy got the coping skills She needed. Tammy stopped taking medication. Her mood swings were hard to deal with. Yet she is living a normal life. She has a beautiful little boy named Donavin. So Bobby is glad to be in touch with the girls. He loves being a grandpa. And it's good for the kids to see their grandpa.

Every Saturday, I couldn't seem to get myself out of bed. I didn't know what was wrong with me. It was as if the whole week had caught up with me. I was so weak. I had no strength, I couldn't even yell. What was wrong with me? In time I find out it's depression. I have been depressed all my life. I never felt this bad. With two little girls to raise. I needed all the help that I can get.

As Tammy got older, she caused me more heart grief and emotional distress. She always seemed to get into a complex situation. Once she said she was riding her bike outside. There was a man in a car driving by. He took out a gun saying hey you, the man showed her a gun. Tammy panicked. She came home and pulled all the shades down. She was hiding, and whispering. So I had to get cell phones for us all so I could keep tabs on the girls. Tammy had a hard time taking her prescribed meds. She would pretend to take the meds, but she wasn't. At times Tammy was really down. I had to get professional help for her. She was following the same path as her brother Tod. Tammy had been in and out of the hospital numerous times. While in the hospital she learned how to make beautiful snowflakes out of paper. No other kids in the treatment program appeared interested in learning how to make them. I was glad that she learned to do something beautiful out of paper.

The day came when Tammy had to move into a Minneapolis treatment place for young girls. There was structure and she was being supervised and watched all the time. Tammy was there for a year. She learned how to cope with her mood swings. If she wanted to that is. Tammy had to do what was the right thing for her to do. She had to want to go forward in her life and not backwards. Tammy needed to use the skills she learned to succeed in life. Tammy had to be bold and do what is right. It was only up to her to doit.

I had to do what was right for us. My doctor gave me a low dose of Paxil to help handle the edge of the depression. I did not want to take medication for depression. Originally I was against taking meds, although I believe I needed the help. Besides, God gave us doctors and medication for a reason. If they help, there is nothing wrong with it. I had to not listen to what other people said about the medication. I shouldn't let people scare me. I had to do what was right for me.

Sometimes the girls got into fighting and quarreling with one another, it was not good. They would break each other's bones. Once, Cassie made a homemade pie. We were saving the pie for after dinner desert. Tammy decided to take a piece before. Cassie got mad and threw the whole pie into Tammy's face. Tammy was crying. She had whipped cream all over her face. We all started laughing, because Tammy looked funny with a face full of pie.

Cassie always seemed to have fun with other girlfriends. She kept very busy in school activities. She also worked part time. I think both girls had a lot of anger in them that needed to come out. At the time I was their mother and the Lord was their father. This was very hard for me physically to accept. To be a single parent, that is. Raising two girls. One had special needs, the other one was very stressed and would worry a lot. I felt like I failed all of my children. At times, I would get so angry that I would take an object like a spatula and hit the wall until the object would break. I was so angry that I cried.

I told the girls that I was going to put them in a foster home. The girls knew I didn't mean the things I said at the time. I told them that I was sorry. Still, I felt bad because of how I acted. When I got upset, I had to do what I thought was right. Maybe the doctor was right. Maybe I did need meds to help me. I had been in depression for too many years, although I never received professional help. I never thought about it. I had previously heard bad things about some types of medication. I was scared to try any. I thought, it is better than doing street drugs. I had to give it a try. I did not want the girls to see how sad I was

I tried to keep myself together. I didn't want the girls to worry about me. Cassie did worry about things. At times we talked about my anger, and things like chasing the girls with a broom. We laughed and laughed. At times we would talk about when I had accidents, then we would have a good time laughing. We would talk about the things Cassie did because she was mad at me. For instance, Cassie hid a piece of my coffee pot so that I couldn't make coffee. Another time Cassie put mouthwash in my body spray bottle. I thought it smelled fresh. It was fresh all right! I had no idea it was mouth wash and not body spray. Later, Cassie told me about it. After I used it, when the bottle was almost gone. Another time Cassie poured water all over my bed. We did do a lot of laughing.

The neighbor thought we were always having parties. It was just us girls having fun.

Eventually, I decided to go on a low dose of medication. I told a friend of mine. She said, "No, don't take them, they are bad for you." So I got scared. I stopped taking the medication before they had a chance to work. I went back to the doctor. He said to me don't you trust me? I said yes. He said give the meds another try. It took a while, then it seemed to help. Then I went up to a higher dose. The meds really did seem to help. I felt glad that now I was receiving help. I was on the road to recovery. After all these years I am still healing.

THE ROAD I LEAD

I know your every need. I know what
you want before you wanted it.
I have placed some of those desires
within you. I will show you what too do.
I am living inactive inside of you.

All that you ask it shall be given onto you.
Just follow the road that I lead.
I lift the load for you as a deed.
That gift is the road I lead.
You are truly in good hands, indeed.

In hopes that you will forever be with me.
This I can agree. Be still follow my lead

Running into the arms of Love

you will be truly grateful to follow my lead
Indeed I will be forever grateful I will stay
faithful follow my lead, follow my lead indeed.

REST, REST, REST

Rest my precious one rest at last.
For I hold the future, the present, the past.
I know when you worry. So give me
your heart. Please don't worry.
I will tell you a story. Rest, rest, rest...

When the sun goes down
It's time to Rest, rest, rest.
Even the birds rest in their nests.
The stars that sleep a certain time.
They know when it's time to rise
and shine. Rest, rest, rest...

The sun sleeps behind the clouds.
Keep in mind there is no doubt or
loose bells. The moon sleeps as well.
This kind of story I like to tell.
Rest, rest, rest...It's time for me to
rest as well. So rest my dearest, rest in me.

So rest my dearest rest at last.
For I hold the present, the future, the past.
My love for you will forever last.
Rest, my little one rest at last,
All these things will come to past.
Rest my little one rest at last.

Chapter Eighteen

ANSWERED PRAYERS

It was great to see answered prayers. Sometimes it took a while, sometimes it didn't. One thing for sure we have to wait. That's the hardest thing to learn is patience. It seems we never stop learning that. These are only a few prayers that God answered out of the many. It's not because I prayed. It's because Jesus was praying with me. It's not something I did. It's because of what the Lord has done.

A little neighbor girl was sick. I made some homemade soup for her. I asked God to heal this girl. My hopes were that when she ate the soup, the Lord would answer my prayer. The next day the girl went back to school. She had no idea that I prayed for her.

Next a young girl had her kidneys collapse and her organs shut down. The church prayed for her. She miraculously was healed. A man needed heart surgery. So he was about to get open heart surgery. When they cut him open they said that this man had nothing wrong with him, he didn't need open heart surgery after all.

Another time I was praying at home. I was on my knees. I had a vision of a woman I knew that was a missionary in Mexico. In this vision the women looked like she was very sad. I asked the Lord, "What is wrong?" I started to pray for this family. Months later they came to town. They said that their daughter had died, but that the Lord raised her from the dead.

I am sure that others were praying for them as well. This was exciting and awesome to be a worker of miracles. This truly is a rewarding ministry.

At times, I needed to pray for a certain group of people for positive reasons throughout the many years and seasons. For instance the Lord had me pray for people with cancer. Then the Lord had me pray for people who are bleeding or that may be hurt.

Once, my older brother fell down the stairs at my niece's house where he was living. Nobody knew that he was unconscious for days. His brain was bleeding. The doctors wanted to do an emergency surgery. I went to the hospital. I took anointed oil. I first asked my brother to pray for salvation. So my brother accepted Jesus in his heart. Then I anointed him and prayed over him. The next day my brother got out of intensive care. They put him in a regular room. He didn't need surgery after all. Praise to the Lord for this wonderful miracle.

Next, I went to the hospital to pray for my mother-in-law Ethel who was 99 years old. She had lost a lot of blood. She needed eight pints of blood. The doctors said she was bleeding inside somewhere and they needed to do exploratory surgery to try to find out where she was bleeding from. So I went to the hospital again. I asked her to pray for salvation, which she did. Then I anointed her with oil. The next day she was out of intensive care. They put her in a regular room. She got to live another year and a half. She was only one month away until her one hundredth birthday when she passed away.

Then I prayed for a man to be healed of hepatitis A, B and C. As I laid hands on this person I asked him if he felt anything. He said yes, he could feel the waves. He meant the Lord was doing a work in him. He could feel the waves of heat rejuvenating his body and the anointing of the Lord. Later I got a praise report. The man had been healed. Praise be to the Lord!

Next I prayed over a woman praying with her eyes closed. She said she felt several hands on her head. Yet it was just my hands. When she opened her eyes, she said she saw an angel by me. That was awesome.

There are many prayers that the Lord has answered. A woman asked me to pray for her. She was battling cancer. When I put my hands on her and prayed for her, she said she felt something. The next time I saw this woman, she told me that she was better. That she had been to the doctor and her numbers were way down. In fact she was completely healed. Now when I see healings and miracles, I get all excited like a little kid in the candy store. To see the movement of god. To be a part of the Lord healing many people, a part of many works of healing and miracles and wonders.

I took training to become a team member in the ministry of the healing rooms. These are only a few testimonies that the Lord has answered. I felt the Lord calling me to this ministry when I decided that I was going to be a part of it. It felt right. I felt like I belong in this ministry. I felt as though this is what I was born to do. To be able to lay hands on people and to see their healing is rewarding. To have someone's appearance change right before your eyes. This is rewarding to see.

Another time another team member and myself prayed for a woman over the telephone. She couldn't bend all the way over. The disc in her back was damaged. She was in much pain. By the time we were going to get off the phone, the women screamed that she was healed. She could actually bend over and touch her toes without any pain. All honor, glory, and praise to the Lord.

My aunt was dying, all her insides were shutting down, and she saw people who had gone to be with the Lord. She said that the Lord wanted her. I got a word of wisdom, a word of knowledge. I told my mother, "It's not her time." Then God gave a miracle, overnight she was healed. Praise God. God is good all the time.

A woman came in for prayer. She could not hear. So I prayed for her. Then I asked, "Can you hear anything?" The women had a little boy with her. He yelled in her ear and asked if she could hear. She wasn't sure what the boy was saying. So I laid hands on this woman again and prayed for her again. Then the boy yelled in her ear again. The woman still wasn't sure if she could understand what the boy was saying. So, again I laid my hands on the woman. Again the boy yelled in her ear. She said yes, she could hear. Only it wasn't too loud. So when the woman left, she wrote down on her clipboard that next time she was going to ask for prayer for her ears. Then I was told to not jump too fast, and say that the woman could hear. But the woman told me she could hear, just not as loud. So in working in the healing rooms, I have learned to not stop praying over the person. Because their healing could still happen. There were many people saying that they had gotten healed. This is truly a rewarding gift to have. I am blessed to have this gift.

My sister Anna went to the hospital to get a hysterectomy done. Then she developed pneumonia and a very high fever. She became very sick. She was on her death bed and in an induced coma. She kept developing more complications while in the hospital. So my sister Vicki called me and asked if anyone told me what happened. I said no. Vicki was crying and scared and said that Anna was not doing good. My niece Elicia called me and said that her and her friend were going to come and get me so that I could go to the hospital to pray for my sister Anna. So me, my niece and a friend went down to the hospital. As we walked down into her hospital room it smelled like death. We prayed for 20 - 30 minutes over my sister and I anointed her with oil. As we were leaving out the door to go home, something told me to go back over there. I started rebuking the devil and the spirit of death to get out of my sister. As I was saying that, my sisters whole body was jumping up in the air and the two girls turned back and saw her body as I prayed over my sister. We were all amazed because something was obviously taking place. My sister then came out of the coma and she got better and better each day and then she got to go home. We had a gathering to show that we were glad she is still alive. I'm blessed to be a part of this wonderful victory that took place in my sisters life. Since then she has prayed that Jesus comes to live in her heart. And I pray that she gets to know the Lord before it is time for her to go. It is a wonderful, satisfying feeling to have knowing your loved one went to live with the Lord.

ANSWERED PRAYERS

The Lord would love it if you plant a seed.
This is what we need indeed.
Answered prayers come by and by.
Don't be so shy to cry! You can talk
divine to the Lord. Know that the
Lord has you on his mind. He can

never be unkind at any time.
He is so divine, he is always on time.
Let your faith shine like a shrine.
The Lord has his best interest for you.
He knows just what to do. He
keeps his eyes on you. He will

sometimes use you as a tool. No
matter what you do, he will be with
you. He will see you through.
In hopes that you will get through.
What he wants you to do? So
keep in mind you are mine. The

Lord has his best interest in mind.
The Lord loves to answer your prayers.
For he cares. So take heed, he knows your
every need. He might take time. It's worth
more than a dime. He's not late, he's great.

He's always on time. Keep in mind you'll
need more than a dime. Answered prayers
are answered in a nick of time. This is
puzzling and always blows my mind?

This is not a shrine. That God
is never late he's always on time.
Without a doubt in my mind.
Please be kind if you don't mind.

Chapter Nineteen

WHEN ANGELS APPEAR

WHEN ANGELS APPEAR

When angels appear I will draw you near
I won't disappear.
You are my dear do not fear I'm here.
I have a plan that's in my hand
for you to follow your whole lifespan.
I will show you what to do.
My dear do not fear. When angels appear.
Stay in gear. Do not tear.
Be of good cheer for you are my dear.
It seems you appear to be sincere.
feel free do not despair I will share.
When angels appear.
I will draw you near you are my dear.
When angels appear do not fear.
I will draw you near.
In hopes that you will draw near to me and me to you.
If I am not there one hundred.

Percent, help will come whom I have sent.
You know I admire you can you tell?
In hopes this is what you desire as well.
This is in my heart I can truly tell.
I will draw you near.
I will not disappear.
You are my dear. Do not fear. For I am here.
So draw near. I will be here.
You are my dear in which I will draw you near.
Do not fear I'm near.
You are my dear in whom I will draw near.
Do I make myself clear? Can you hear?
Oh dear! Do not smear what is near.
Please be a dear.
Do not fear for the time of my return is near.

Running into the arms of Love

I remember a time when Tod was little. I was holding his hand. We were getting ready to cross a very busy street called Robert Street. There was no trace of wind that day. As we were about to cross, a big gush of wind pushed us both back onto the curb of Robert Street in Saint Paul. As we both looked up, we saw a big semi-truck whizzing past, almost hitting us. We both knew that this was the hand of the Lord.

Later in life when my family and I rode bikes around the Twin Cities, the Lord was watching over us as usual. Once, while I was ridding my bike. I was crossing the street, the light changed. Some young kids were driving in a car. They could not stop in time to keep from hitting me. They screamed. It was unreal, as if a big invisible hand stopped their car. Everyone was in shock. I knew that it was the Lord and his angels.

When it came time for me to ride my bike across the bridge, I couldn't bring myself to do it. Bobby was getting mad at me because I would start to go across the bridge, then I would stop because I was frantic and so afraid. I couldn't bring myself to go across the bridge, no matter how hard I tried. The same thing happened when I tried to cross the street, even if the light was green. I couldn't bring myself to cross the street. The light kept changing. Bobby was mad at me again. After a long while I finally got the nerve to cross. This took time and patience, a lot of patience.

There was a time when I fell off my bike and landed into a manhole. There were many other times I could have died as well. Once I flew off my bike and into a swamp. My leg was stuck under the handle bars of the bike. And I couldn't move. So there I was, drowning in two feet of swamp water. When I got home my nurse's assistant started laughing at me, asking me what had happened? I told her I had gone for a swim in the swamp. I smelt like the swamp I looked funny. As if I was a swamp creature. We had a good laugh. I don't know how my leg got unstuck, I don't recall how I got out of that situation. It was the Lord again. The Lord has been there all along.

Once I had very little laundry soap left and I had no money to buy additional laundry soap. The Lord made that laundry soap last a long time.

It lasted for many months, close to a year. I couldn't believe it. Yet I had to, because it was really happening to me. How sweet, God stretched the quantity of soap to last. What an awesome God.

Another time when Tod was little, he was playing with fire and had started something on fire. I began to panic. I didn't know where the smoke and blaze was coming from. Hours later I found a burnt blanket near some curtains. The fire had been miraculously put out. Now that was a miracle. The duplex was old, it should have burnt down. I believe it was the Lord or some of his angels to aide us again. Another incident happened when my mom needed a long winter coat to cover her legs when she walked to work. I took all my bus money that I had and bought her a long jacket from a thrift store that I lived next door to. When I went into my top drawer dresser I found a whole pile of change in my drawer. I believe that the Lord or an angel was sent to put this money in the drawer. No human person could have come into my house to put this money into my dresser drawer.

Another time I didn't have to pay my phone bill for six months. I kept getting notices that I had credit because I overpaid. I never questioned it because I knew this was the working of the Lord. Once I looked into the refrigerator, and I had an inch of milk in the container. When I went back to the refrigerator later I had almost a full gallon. I kept rubbing my eyes thinking that I was seeing things. On a rainy day I had no umbrella. The Lord had it rain everywhere but on me. This happened a few times. I feel special and blessed. I've been told that I am the Lord's pet. I sure feel like I am at times. I love the Lord. He is so good all the time. Sometimes I would cry with joy for all the wonderful things that the Lord was doing. If I had twenty-five cents, the Lord multiplied it, turning it into twenty-five dollars. All kinds of blessings the Lord was doing for me and my family's life.

My baby sister was attacked by four or five guys. She fought them as best she could. One of the guys that attacked her had an axe. They were going to use it on my sister's head. The guy hit my sister on the head. A miracle happened, the sharp edge did not hit her head. God was looking out for my sister. Somebody was praying for her. I knew it was Jesus interceding on behalf of my sister. God had mercy on my sister. I was praying along with the Lord.

For many years I have prayed for various people, sometimes I never got to meet the people I prayed for. One day I believe I will see them. It has been a rewarding feeling to see the many people receive their healings. To see people leave positively different then when they originally came is rewarding. To see their countenance change before your eyes. This is beautiful to see. Now I sense what a doctor must feel. The sense of accomplishment. Helping someone. Seeing them receive their special healing is a wonderful feeling. Now that's what it is all about.

When people come to the healing rooms for prayer, we have them fill out a piece of paper on a clip board chart that has information about that person. The chart information will say are they saved? Are they baptized in the Holy Spirit? What church are they affiliated with? How did they hear about the healing rooms? We also ask are you under the care of a professional doctor? The chart will also ask what you would like prayer for. It could be emotionally, physically, mentally, or spiritually. There are two to three team members in a room with a guest. We lay our hands over the clip board. We pray for that person before they enter the room, before we meet them. The Lord will show and reveal to us what the person needs prayer for. Sometimes the person doesn't know why they have come in for prayer. We tell the person what they may need prayer for. Beforehand, when the Lord reveals this to us about the person, they normally are shocked and surprised, impressed, very relieved. And very grateful that they came in for prayer. Some marvel, some are very excited to see what happens and what the Lord has for them. At times this can get a little hard if the person is in denial to receive what you have to say. And sometimes it is scary if the person has a demon in them. Then you are fighting the devil in disguise. Then again, we have to be strong because "greater is He that is in me than he that is in this world." It's wonderful when team members work together, the gifts flow and the Lord brings unity so that we all work together. The people receive what they need.

Each time I had a baby, my health declined. I developed arthritis on both of my knees. I then developed asthma. I would breathe funny. The kids would say, "Are you okay mom?"

I would say, "Yea, why?"

They would say, "Because you are breathing funny." I didn't notice. Although I did notice at times I was out of breath. From time to time when I breathed, I made a wheezing noise. I also developed fibromyalgia. So I had pain of some sort daily. I don't know what it is like to not have pain. I also have a bone spur on my big toe. This feels like a broken toe. I got a cortisone shot to help me with the pain. It's a good thing I didn't pass out just looking at the shot. My toe got worse before it felt better. It turned all black and blue and purple. The doctor says I can only have three of these shots in my life time. From time to time I take pain pills. I try not to take them. I then developed plantar fasciitis. My heel hurt so very bad. I had to wear tennis shoes *24n* and have heel lifts in my shoe. In time the Lord healed this from me. I now could wear slippers around the house and sandals in the summer. This was real healing. I was excited and happy. Sometimes I need a little help, to bare the aches and pains. I then developed a bunion on my toe. So I went to the podiatrist and he was trying to find out why I was having pains in my big toe. He kept coming up with ideas about what was wrong. I went to see him a couple times. Three years later I was still in excruciating pain so I went back to see him again. That's when I found out I had a bunion. I had surgery to fix the problem. They put a screw in my big toe to help fuse the bones together. Then recovery was not good. I developed an infection and kept on stubbing my toe. Also, I was wearing sandals that was rubbing on my toe where the screw was located. Then the screw moved and my bones did not fuse. This caused an infection. I went back to the doctor and he said that if the infection didn't clear they would have to amputate my toe and possibly my whole foot. I had to have a second surgery on the same toe. They removed the screw and put in wires to help fuse the bones together. They gave me a knee scooter to get around with because they didn't want me to walk on that foot. It took a while for it to heal but thank God that it healed so that I didn't have to have my toe or foot amputated. It was a scary thing to possibly have my foot amputated. So I prayed over my foot and toe. My friends were praying as well. My God answered our prayer and healed me. I went back to the doctor and he said they were fusing but not all the way yet. I went back a month later and he took another xray and said the bones were fused and took out the wires. This was good news to hear. The Doctor flicked my toe. And that was a true confirmation that my toe was healed. Healing at last!

I will keep doing what the Lord has called me to do. I feel that's why I am here. Everybody has a reason why they are here. Everybody has a job and a purpose. I am sure that I am doing what I was born to do. There were many miracles that took place in my life over the years. I've seen many things in my lifetime. It's great to be able to look and see who and what I am praying for. To be able to lay hands on that person. It's wonderful to see the marvelous works of the Lord. What a mighty God we have indeed. Answered prayers are a blessing to have.

I have had many CAT scans done over the years for the brain injury, and also to see if the bullet is still in its place or if it has moved from the original spot. Every time it appears people are amazed that I am walking around with a partial bullet still in my brain.

One of the most recent times I was having a CAT scan done, the young radiology man ran out of the room to where I was laying down in the donut tube getting the test done. He came running up to me. He said, "Do you have steel in your ear?" I said no. He seemed freaked. He said that he saw some steel fragments coming out of my ear. I believe after all these years the partial bullet has been deteriorating, and fragments of the partial bullet were coming out little by little. I believe the Lord has been miraculously deteriorating the remaining partial bullet, healing me in the process.

It now appears that I don't have headaches every day or as frequently as I used to. However, they seem to come at a certain time of the year. At times, I do get severe headaches 24-7. I still get dizzy spells from time to time. The headaches have come in different forms. It could be shooting pain. It could feel like a migraine, it could hurt so bad that I couldn't lift my head up. They could be so severe that I couldn't move. Sometimes it felt as if a rubber band was squeezing my forehead. At times I had dizzy spells. I would bump my head hard or I would fall down. At other times, the back of my head hurt as if I got hit on the head. Now this is only happening after 36-years. All in all it is better all around.

Once the dizzy spells were severe. I could not leave the house. Sometimes I would scream because I didn't like the feeling of being dizzy.

I also do things crooked. My writing goes uphill. My picture hanging is crooked. Everything I do, looks crooked. I also have a hard time seeing the difference in sizes of things. I was at my mother's house. They put a frozen pie into the toaster oven. I could have sworn I saw the pie getting bigger. I told my brother, "It's getting bigger."

So my brother looked. He said, "It's not getting bigger." It's sometimes hard for me to go onto elevators or escalators. I try not to make a scene in public. The dizzy spells can become dangerous at times. Now days, I believe I am doing better thanks to the Lord. What a blessing. The Lord is still healing me in every way.

I also have depth perception problems which is not being able to see how close things really are. This is a side effect of having only one eye. I also am color blind. Talk about problems, I think I have a lot. I deal with one thing at a time. Sometimes I get overwhelmed. Then I began to walk around in circles, and then I have anxiety attacks.

The Bible says in Proverbs 17:22 that laughing is good medicine for your heart. A broken spirit dries the bones. I believe that I've had many miracles concerning my heart. I have had mild to severe chest pain in the past. As I was overly stressed at times. The paramedics came and took me to the hospital a few times. By the time the doctors treated me, I appeared all better. The only thing they found at the time was that my heart beats irregularly. This is not normal. Then again, I am not your normal person. I am a peculiar person. I belong to Jesus.

I count my blessings every day. Thank God he's there for us. Even if it seems He isn't, He is. I am thankful for how far I have come. I know things could have been a lot worse in life. I have a lot to be thankful for.

When Tod got sick with the chickenpox, in the wee hours he developed a very high fever. He was hallucinating, playing with his toys and talking out loud to someone that was not there. Shortly after Tod saw an angel in his doorway. The angel had a sword of fire in their hand like they were guarding the doorway. I believe Tod really did see this angel. Later Tod was rushed to a twenty-four hour emergency hospital in Saint Paul. There he was looked at. The doctor said thatTod could have damaged his liver from the high fever.

There were times when I had self-pity and guilt. I would blame myself for everything that went wrong in my life as well as my children's lives. I had to learn how to stop blaming myself for these things. Romans 8:1: "Therefore know no condemnation to them which are in Christ Jesus. Who walk not after the flesh, but after the Spirit."

Many years have gone by. Tod had grown into a strong man. He was always curious about his father. He wondered what he looked like. This has been a dream for Tod to see and meet his father. His whole life.

Tod's grandma had a picture of his father and me. She only had one and she gave it to Tod. Tod wanted to meet him. In person. Yet he was scared to meet him. Tod wanted to know about his fathers side of the family. He was curious of his heritage. Tod wanted to find himself as to where he belonged. He wanted to know some of his family. When we had gatherings. Tod felt misplaced. Tod said that some of my family members gave him a dirty look. Tod still had this desire to see his father. And maybe one day meet some more of his family on his fathers side. Many more years go by. Tod had met his half brother on Facebook. Then Tod found out that he had three more brothers. So Tod was very happy to know that he had a few other brothers. So Tod meets one of his brothers. That lived a few hours away from Tod. So they get together and meet one another. Tod is very happy and exited to meet one of his brothers. Soon after Tod meets the other brothers on Facebook. They all welcome Tod into the family. Tod finds out more about his family. He is excited to find things out about his family. Tod's older brother remembers things from the past like when the swat team got a hold of Phil while he was staying with Jenny at night. His brother also remembers Phil telling them about the letter he got from Tod. Tod said oh so he did get my letter while he was in prison. Tod called his dad a coward. He said that his dad could of at lease let him know that he got his letter. Tod's aunt meets Tod on Facebook. Tod is happy to get in touch with her. They talk on the phone all the time. I remember when Tod was a baby. His aunt came to see him. She brought a Christmas gift for Tod. Tod gets discouraged. His brothers don't have time for him. Maybe in time they could take time for one another. For now healing is still taking place in Tod's heart. For feeling rage, hate, envy, jealously that the other brothers got to know their father. Not Tod. Tod talked to his father, his father all ready lied to him. Phil told Tod that Tod was going to get sick of him calling him everyday. Tod told his dad that he wanted to meet him. Phil said that Tod waited his whole life he can wait longer. Tod hasn't heard from Phil for a long time. Tod lost Phil's number. So now it is up to Phil to get in touch with Tod if he wants to be in Tod's life. And if he doesn't, there is no loss because their was nothing there to began with. Tod feels rejected not only by his father, but also by me. I can understand where Tod is coming from.

Phil and Tod get together a few times. Also talk on the phone. Once Tod brings his gun. To show his father. Phil's eyes widen big. He was startled. That Tod had a gun. Because Phil did not know his son. And his son doesn't know him. I can imagine, how Phil felt. For a moment. That maybe Tod wanted to get revenge. For destroying our lives. So Tod don't hear from his father or brothers. Tod feels sad. This makes him feel lonesome and depressed. I told Tod don't let it get him down. Because he will hear from them sometime.

YOU ARE MINE

I hear your every prayer. Be near
to me won't you dare? I am with
you everywhere. You must know
that I care. You dust the snare of
every care; that you cannot bear.
Go ahead let yourself near. Won't
You dear? If you know that I care.

This I can bear, don't try it on your own.
This will take you till you're grown.
I must be discreet. While you lay
at my feet. This we can beat! Retreat,
what a blessed treat. Now isn't that
sweet? So be neat until we meet
Now that's neat. Please be sweet.

You can't look back. That's what gets you down. If I keep looking to the sunny future, I get excited and happy inside. If I have an attitude of gratitude, I will keep looking ahead. I will try to focus on the good things. Because there are good things for all of us. What seems to help you through difficult times? It helps me to have a sense of humor.

I want to tell you the story of a rooster. It was late during the wee hours. I could hear a rooster. I was thinking a rooster was on my apartment patio. So I got out of bed and ran to the sliding patio doors and looked out. Then I went back to bed. Then I heard the rooster again. So I got up and ran to the patio doors again. I looked out I did not see a rooster. My cats were lined up, looking out the patio glass door. Each time I got up and ran to the patio doors, the cats looked at me like I was crazy. Then I went back to bed. A little while later I heard the rooster again. Then I got up for the third time coming to the patio doors. I had live geese and deer come up to my patio doors. Sometimes the cats were entertained by birds or rabbits or squirrels. In our space outside. For a while Bah Bah my cat was catching rabbits. I didn't let Bah Bah outside any more. It was safer to keep him in the house. So I naturally thought that there was a rooster on our patio. So I went back to bed. Later that day I told my daughter about the rooster event. My younger daughter said, Mom that was not a rooster. That was my alarm clock."

I later called my mom, and told her about the rooster story. For a while, whenever I saw my mom, she would look at me and say, "That darn rooster." Then we would laugh.

Next I'll tell you about one of my experiences at McDonald's. I'd never previously been to this particular McDonald's location. One day I went to McDonald's with my male friend. I ordered my food, and then went to sit down waiting for my friend to bring the food. As I was sitting, I observed around me a band of mirror, surrounded by plants. I turned and looked and saw someone wearing the same jacket as me. I thought to myself, I wonder if the person I saw in the mirror had gotten their jacket at Target as I had. Then I observed this person was wearing the same color shirt as I was. I thought to myself, I don't want to be dressed like someone else in public. So then I decided to get a closer look to see what this person looked like. I lifted my head up then down. Then did it again. I couldn't find their head. Then I realized that the reason why I couldn't find their head is because it was me. I couldn't believe that this other person was me! I didn't know that there was a piece of mirror there. I only saw plants. No wonder I couldn't see the persons' head. As my friend brought our food to the table, I was laughing so hard. My friend asked me, "Aren't you going to eat?" I tried to tell them why I was laughing. However, he couldn't understand me because I was laughing so hard. I tried telling him why I was laughing. The sad thing is I actually believed that there was another woman at McDonald's dressed just like me. I sure got a good laugh! Two guys came into McDonald's, one of the guys was bald with tattoos on his bald head. The guys must have thought I was laughing at them. They must have thought I was on drugs at the time. Anyways that's one of my experiences at MC Donald's.

You've got to have a sense of humor. If you can keep your joy that's great. If you need help to forgive, ask God to help you to forgive. This will also help tremendously. You will heal so you won't have bitterness, resentment or unforgiveness. If you don't get rid of these resentful things they will choke you up and destroy you. That's what the Bible says! Mathew 13:22 "He also that received seed among the thorns is he that hear the word and the care of this world and the deceitfulness of riches choke the word and he becomes unfruitful." If you have a sense of humor that's great. You stand a better chance of getting the healing you may need.

For instance when I did my family's laundry, I would put the socks together attempting to match one with the other. To make a pair I would attempt to put the colored socks together that were not the same color. Once, I hung one of my family member's sweat pants on a hanger, thinking it was a sweater. Weeks went by. My family member couldn't find their sweat pants. All along they were hanging in the closet shaped like a sweater.

Got to have a sense of humor. There's plenty more where these stories came from. I have had some good laughs! As for my language, I fluently speak English. However, sometimes I pronounce words wrong. Some find it amusing or unique because of the way I talk. For instance, for the particular day of the week, Thursday, it sounds like I am saying, 'thirsty.' The word, 'vegetarian' I would pronounce as veterinary. The word, 'karaoke,' I would pronounce it "carry o' key." If I said I need to iron my pants, I'd pronounce one word wrong: I need to onion my pants! I order food at the restaurant. I order "tragedienne Alfredo." My daughter says, "Ma, they don't have such a thing here, where are you getting the letter G from? They have fettuccine Alfredo." My children laugh with me from time to time. Because I appeared silly sometimes to them. If I used the wrong words, it was funny to them. If I wanted a sliver of a cake, I would pronounce one word wrong again. Can I have a slipper of cake? So not only do I pronounce the word wrong, I also sometimes say the wrong word instead. I intend to say, 'I want my pillow,' but I say, 'I want my pickle' instead. Yes, we've all had our hard times growing up. However, we laugh and have fun years later. After all, one thing for sure. It's good to be in the arms of love. Another thing I have a habit of doing. And that is I count things all the time. Sometimes I count by ones. Sometimes I count by twos. If I am outside. And there are geese, or birds or what ever I see I count them. Over and over. If I am at the Doctor's office. I count the squares on the celling over and over. If I am at the kids school I count the artwork hanging up over and over. Where ever I am I will find something to count over and over. I can't say that I count sheep over and over because I can't sleep. Maybe I am tired of counting so I don't have trouble falling asleep at night. All though I do take amitritpyline to help with going into a deep sleep. Also helps with fibromyalgia. This helps the pain that I have in my neck. I get this probably from tilting my head more to the left side because I can't see out of my right eye. Through all the years I have learned to be thankful and greatful for what I have. And not for what I loss. To be Thankful in any circumstance Or situation. That I should take one day at a time. Because if it is God's will it will be done in his time. I Should not rush into anything. Or try to hurry God. I have to rest in him. When I do I have peace and contentment. When I trust the Lord 100 % and not 50 or 75% I eliminate many necessaries. In my life. Such as pain, anxiety, paranoia, confusion, fear, doubt, instability,

Which leads to poor decision making which leads to danger which leads to death. You pay a price for not trusting God. In any and every situation. Our loss and the evil's gain. I continue to pray for people that I don't know stranger's. If I hear somebody use God's name in vain. I ask God to forgive them because they don't know what they are doing. Same if someone swears or cruses. Life is too short to spend it foolishly.

Chapter Twenty

SPRINGS OF JOY

SPRINGS OF JOY

Like a kid that gets a new toy that brings him
lots of joy. When you see someone in need,
and you do God's deed. When you give someone
laughter and you laugh about it the day after.
When you trust and obey, for there's no other way.
When you tend to believe, you will begin to receive.
When you began to shout without a doubt. When
You give and don't receive. You will be truly relieved.
When you give of your time. You began to shine.
To me that's springs of joy. Like a kid that gets a
new toy that brings them lots of joy.

Cassie kept getting sinus infections. She practically lived on antibiotics. I took her to the Ear, Nose and Throat specialist. Eventually, she got her adenoids removed and her nasal sinuses scraped so she could breathe easier. The sinus infections ceased after that.

Tammy got a sore throat. Then Cassie got a sore throat. Then I got a sore throat. The doctor said that we all had to get our tonsils out. We were experenceing a brady Bunch episode. Tammy was supposed to go to Valley

Fair with her friends. She had to cancel. However, she wanted to go. She said she didn't feel good enough to go. Tammy was the first to get her tonsils out. Next in line was me. Cassie was the last to get her tonsils out. When Cassie got her surgery done, I was still recovering from my surgery.

The nurse said to me that I did not look good. So the nurse had me lay down on a hospital bed. So there were Cassie and I, side by side. The staff gave us a list of things we could eat that wouldn't hurt our throat much. Everything they said we could have burned our throats. I had a box of world famous chocolate candy bars. Cassie decided to eat them all up! Cassie claimed that the chocolate was the only thing that soothed her throat. Tammy was scared to even swallow her own saliva, so she spit inside of a Kleenex instead of swallowing. She used quite a few boxes of Kleenex.

I met a man from church, his name was Sid. He said he had once met me at my friend's house when I had really long hair. Sid said that he had thought to himself, that I was the kind of girl he would like to marry. Years went by. I forgot about meeting Sid. Then I started going to the same church that Sid and some other friends of ours went to. We were sitting next to each other in church. I didn't remember meeting him before at a different time and place. One day we just hit it off. When church was over, we still were talking to each other. Sid was shy; he usually did not talk to many women. So we hit it off. Sid took the girls and me out to eat. At the time the girls were misbehaving. Sid was embarrassed, so was I. The girls took off their shoes in the restaurant. They acted like they owned the place. The girls acted like wild children. I did not realize they would act that way in public.

Sid and I started dating on a regular basis. The girls seemed to like him. We eventually got engaged. We got a license to get married. Soon we were planning our wedding day. The pastor was counseling us to prepare us for marriage. It was called premarital counseling. Around this time another couple was also engaged to get married. So there were to be two weddings coming up. I bought the girls their wedding clothes, shoes and all. Time went on we were all excited about the two wedding events coming up! I then got cold feet. I gave the ring back to Sid. It hurt to do it. However, I thought I was doing the right thing. Sid and I broke up. Then we got back together over time as we got engaged for the second time. We had to buy a new marriage license because the other one had expired. The time was getting closer to our wedding date. I got scared again. So we postponed the wedding for the second time.

I was in the process of moving. The thing was, I didn't know where I was moving to. I gave my notice. I could not find a place that I could afford at the time. Then I told Sid, lets' get married. Then the girls and I would be able to have a place to live. At the time Sid had a house and lived in it with his mother. Sid agreed with me.

It came time to get dressed for the wedding. Tammy said to me, "Mom these shoes don't fit me." I told her that they would be fine, that she just had to break them in. Poor girl, she wore them with her heels hanging out of her shoes. I looked at Tammy. I said, "Tammy what are you doing wearing those shoes, they are too small."

Tammy said to me, "Mom I tried to tell you the shoes were too small."

I said to Tammy "If I didn't listen, you should have shown me." Tammy's feet had grown since Sid and I had got engaged the first time.

It seems Cassie had troubles with her shoes as well. When Cassie went to Early Education, she had two left tennis shoes. I looked down and I saw her feet. Hmm two left feet. I then switched her shoes around. I looked again. Cassie still had two left shoes. At first I thought that my eye was playing tricks on me. I thought to myself what is going on? I just fixed her shoes. Well no wonder. Cassie had two left tennis shoes that were the same kind of tennis shoes. This was very unusal. I hoped nobody else noticed.

Every morning the ladies and parents had a little snack or treat. This was the first time I ever had a bagel with cream cheese. Today I still like them.

Sid and I kept our wedding plans as scheduled. We didn't have our pastor marry us. At the time Sid and I were switching churches. So we had a different reverend marry us at his personal house of residence. We were going to have only a few people. The house got full and packed with people. For many years people have waited for Sid to get married. Sid has had a lot of roommates. They all had gotten married. A woman at church said to me, "It's like God brought you here for Sid. Sid thought that maybe he would have to stay single for the remainder of his life. Surprise, surprise! Then I came along. Sid had an already made family. Sid's mother was against him getting married the first time. The second time she accepted it. I believe she enjoyed being a mother n law. She liked having a daughter n law. She called me her daughter. She also loved being a grandma to my kids. Ethel and I would have fun in the kitchen, talking and laughing together. Ethel was a lot of fun. She and I seemed to get along better than Sid and me. At times we played cards. Some times we would be in the \ kitchen all day. I would do the baking and cooking. Ethel would sit and talk with me. Sometimes she did her puzzles. She kept me company.

Things began to happen that were not good. Sid would do little things that added up to no good. He chased the girls around the house like a crazy guy. When he caught up with them he put them high up against the wall and screamed at them. Sid took his 99 year old mother and shook her up screaming at her. He took a hair brush and hit me on the butt with it. Because I would not let him cut my hair. I knew that things would only get worse. Then Sid jumped up and down while having a temper tantrum just like a little kid. I couldn't believe what I saw. I began to have seizures, it was not epilepsy. I was in the hospital for two weeks. I found out I have post-traumatic stress disorder. Now I had no choice. I had to be on antidepressant pills. Eventually the girls and I had to leave. Sid was becoming more physically and verbally abusive.

The girls and I left, ending up in a shelter home. We lived there for a few months. We did get an apartment two months later. I remained separated from my husband Sid for six years. After 6 years we had decided that we would give our marriage a chance. For the six years we were separated we were always together for church Bible studies and so on. We just got along better when we didn't live together. We knew we should get marriage counseling so we could move back together.

Our pastor and his wife gave us marriage counseling. The day was coming that we would reunite together. As husband and wife. Some friends from church who worked in Mexico came to work in Minnesota. This is where they are from. During summer they came here and worked in the healing rooms. When winter came they went back to Mexico and worked in the healing rooms in Mexico. They were the founders of this ministry. I felt the Lord tugging on my heart. Telling me to take the training to work in the healing rooms.

I asked Sid if he would consider taking the classes with me. He really didn't want to. I convinced him to take training with me. We became team members of the healing rooms of Saint Paul. Sid and I remained faithful and committed to the healing rooms. There were times when it was slow. I felt discouraged. Yet we stood faithful. Our friends said that at times they wouldn't have opened if Sid and I didn't come.

In time I talked Sid into being the leader. This took time. The day came when Sid did take the lead. I told him I knew that he had gifts. It was wonderful to see the Lord use us for his Glory. This was a very exciting ministry. The more we were faithful the more God used us and increased our gifts. This was exciting. What I mean by taking the lead is that we have 2 to 3 team members work together in a room. One will start praying and ministering to the guest while the other 2 pray in the spirit, then someone could get a scripture or a vision or a word. We all work together in unity. Everyone shares their gifts. Then guests receive their healing or a word. Something that they needed.

I eventually found an apartment located in West Saint Paul. The two girls and I began once more to rebuild our lives together again. We met new faces and new friends. At the time I could not bring myself to get a divorce. I had been divorced twice already. I didn't want to do it again. So Sid and I became separated most of our early married life. We both decided to try to make our marriage work. As long as we have the Lord I know we can do it. Where there is a will there is a way. As the old saying goes, we do bring joy to one another. Sid and I were seperated for six years. After that

Sid came back to live with me. We lived together for over a year and then suddenly Sid passed. He died in his sleep and it was over.

Five years after Sid passed I began receiving requests on Facebook from men to be friends. The first guy was in Texas we texted each other for hours at a time. I couldn't believe it. I felt like I fell in love with this man. I told this man that I feel like I fell in love with him. He said wow really? Time went on we still text-ed each other. His profile picture looked like it wasn't a real photo. It almost look like a picture from a magazine. This man was very handsome. He said that his wife and him were not together anymore. That he had a five year old daughter. Then in another conversation he said that his daughter was three years old. This man wanted to give me money even if we didn't know each other. Or even if we never met each other. I told him that I couldn't take money from a stranger. He sad please don't say no. But I had to say no. I caught this man in a few lies. When I confronted this man he said you are-mistaken. So I let it go. Then I caught this man lieing to me again. When I told him about it, he tried to deny it. Then he took himself off of Facebook. The second man I befriended was a man in a different country. After a very short time this man asked me to marry him. So I said yes because I was lonesome and lonely. This man wanted me to send him money to fly where I live. This was going to be a lot of money. Three thousand and two hundred dollars. I said no thanks I am not even going to try to go there. If I had him fly where I am I would be stuck with a man I don't even know. And possibly not even like. The way I see it I would have boughten this man. Then he would want to live off of me. Because he said he wanted a wife so that he could retire. So I told this man that I could not marry him. This man was hurt so he says. He said how could I do this to him. That he never thought that I would do this to him. Next guy I just didn't want to talk to him anymore. Next guy he was very controlling. Because he had women that cheated on him he thought all women did. So basically this man treated me like I was a criminal. I went to church and this man kept texting me and asking me am I home yet? When I told him where I was he said oh really like I was lying. I didn't like how this man was treating me. He wanted me to get married and to take care of him and his daughter. I had enough. I said I cant be with him. And that I didn't like the way he treated me. So I said goodbye. Next I meet a man that's years younger than me. We texted each other for a while. This man wanted me to marry him. He says that he has a daughter and that he wanted me to be her mother. I felt comfortable talking to this man. I felt safe with this man. Than he asked me for my personal information. This man was planing to do identity theft. Then this man texted me something that he was suppose to send to another women. So he got busted. He got caught. This man tried to convince me that I got him all wrong. He was just lying. Sad thing, three of these men had daughters. It seems they all had a story.

We have met many different people that have come into our lives. I still keep praying for the people who may need it. We all could use prayer. As we look upon the future with a positive attitude, good things may happen. I have learned to put up with what I can't change, and change what I can. With springs of joy through all the years. I have had a lot of different surgeries. And operations. The Lord gave me strength each time. And the healing processes were tremendously quick. I had to get a hysterectomy. My mother, brother and husband Sid were there with me. This was a good feeling that somebody cared. My doctor sent me some flowers. I truly got blessed. I knew this was the best thing for me and my health. I was glad I didn't have to have any more periods. I am a child of God. The Lord cares about every little thing, about all our every concern. There's nothing too big or too small or too silly for the Lord. He cares about our every need our every want.

Chapter Twenty-One

INCLINATION

INCLINATION

Incline your ears to me. So you may
hear what I want you to hear. Incline
yourself to me. Take your time don't
Waste any time. So wine and dine.
Have a good time. Incline your

tongue too me. That you may be
Strong for me. Incline your lips and hips.
That you may have some kicks.
That I will fix. Be silent, don't be defiant.
Incline your mind to me. Everything

will be fine indeed. Incline your whole self
To me. That you may be what I want you to be.
That everyone may see that I am in you.
You are in me. This is for all men to see.
Incline yourself to me...

The Lord had me run into animals that needed homes. I would try to find a home for them. Then the next thing I know, I am pet sitting. It first started when I took care of a bunny rabbit that was barely alive. One of my younger daughter's friends didn't know how to take care of the bunny. The poor bunny was malnourished. The bunny was unsanitary and dirty. The bunny was kept in a cardboard box. The box was covered in nasty drippings of urine and rabbit drippings. I felt so bad for the bunny. The bunny couldn't even hop, or walk. I bought a cage for the bunny. I got everything ready for the bunny. In eight days the bunny gained weight. The bunny could walk, run, and play with the cats. They chased each other around the house. It was cute to watch. The bunny was very happy. I named the bunny Bonnie. Bonnie only lived eight days. Then she died. I know she died happy.

I then got a dwarf bunny, her name was Emily and I called her Emmy. She was little gray bunny. She is called a dwarf bunny because she was full grown but she would always stay small. She lived a few years then she died. Then I took care of a hamster, which we ended up keeping. By the time I knew it, I had a whole family of different hamsters. Then I took a few kittens that were from the humane society. I ended up keeping them.

Next a neighbor got a kitten from their family member. They did not know how to care for the cat. They were afraid of the cat. All the cat wanted to do is play. They mistreated this cat. The lady went knocking on each apartment door, asking if anyone wanted to buy a cat. She came to my door. I said I have enough pets already. Then I found out that they threw the kitten out in the balcony all night long. The kitten was crying. I felt so sad when I found out. If I had known that they were going to put him out on the balcony, or that they were afraid of the kitty, or that they didn't know how to care for the animal, I would have taken him right away. I went knocking on their door and asking if I could have the kitten. The lady said that her sister was coming to get the cat. This was not good. Her sister's kids killed the kitten's sister. I did not want them to hurt or kill this baby kitten. Some how I had to protect this baby kitten. I did not want the kitten to be mistreated anymore. I said to the lady. Can I please have the kitten? I said I don't have any money, but I would care for the kitten.

The lady said I would be doing her a favor. Today that kitten is a young man whose name is Baby Luke. Just think, Luke had a loving good home waiting for him right next door. Who would of thought? Luke is spoiled. But then all my pets are. That's okay. They are so cute to watch. He had a teddy bear that he loved. He would carry the stuffed bear around the house with him. At times he took the bear under the bed with him. I showed people that came to my house his bear. So baby Luke would take it under the bed and hide it. So that I wouldn't show it to people that came over. When baby Luke was getting something to eat Then he dragged the bear to the bowl of food. Face down. As if he wanted the bear to eat. It was the cutist thing ever! At times baby Luke hid under my bed spread you could see a lump in the middle of the bed. I wondered if he did that where he came from. I only hoped that baby Luke felt safe.

I got a white rat named Blanco, he was funny at times. My grandson helped me to not be afraid of the rat. I thought the rat's tail was disgusting. Then again I had to overcome some fears. Then I took care of a little mouse named Buttercup. He belonged to one of my daughters. Buttercup would bite Tammy. she asked if I wanted to take care of it. So I took it. And Buttercup was so cute. I would put my arm into the cage, then Buttercup would climb up my arm, using my arm as if it were a ladder. I let Buttercup crawl all over my shirt. Buttercup would leave his drippings on my shirt. I loved talking to Buttercup. He would watch me as I talked. There were times I couldn't wait to get home from church so that I could take Buttercup out of the cage. One day Buttercup fell off my shoulder. It was a long ways down to the floor for a little mouse. Buttercup was okay. A few days later, Buttercup died. I cried so much, I gave myself a headache. I loved little Buttercup. I felt kind of silly crying over a little mouse. I really loved that little mouse. At least he went happy.

Next I took care of a cat whose family was going through transition. Then the cat's family got their living worked out. In the end the family took their cat back. In the meanwhile, their cat got sick. He misses my cat. Next I take care of a kitten whose family was going on vacation. This is the first time I saw a real copycat. This cat watched my cat then copy what my cat did. This was very cute to watch. Next I get a ferret named socks she is a girl. She belonged to the mainance man. He could not give the care that socks needed. Because this man worked long hours. The reason her name was socks is because she would steel your socks. This was the ferrets name when she was given to me. When my daughter Cassie came home she would take her socks and shoes off and throw them on the floor. My daughter Cassie always took off her socks and shoes when she came home. This was one bad habit that she had. If she wanted any socks she was going to have to learn to pick up her socks before Socks got them. So Socks was a blessing, and she was cute. This man worked for the company that rented the apartments tenants lived in. next I take care of a ferret named scrappy. While his owners find a place to live. So socks had a live in play mate. Scrappy was cute and he had a great personality. Boy did my house stink, it reeked. The ferrets had a grand time. They took my books off the bookshelf. I would let them out of the cage so they would run around and play. They had a lot of fun. They got into mischief.

I have had many incidents in which the Lord was there protecting me. I loved all kinds of animals. I took care of a giant African centipede whose owner did not want to take care of it. They were starving the creature. I felt bad for the creature. So I took care of it. If I put my mind to it I could hold it without freaking. I then gave it to a store called Pet co so they could find it a good home.

In time the one ferret went to his family. Then it was Socks. Later I cared for a cat and her five babies. It was fun to watch them grow. I then I started caring for cats, which ended up being mine for keeps in the end. Meanwhile I think I'll hold off on caring for any other animals except my own. It has been expensive and busy, yet rewarding.

Next a woman came knocking on each door asking if somebody wants a cat. The woman was going to take it to the Humane Society. I felt bad for this cat. He wasn't being treated right. The woman said that this cat would hide under the bed all day. Then when everybody was sleeping at night, the cat would come out. This cat was a white Persian cat, with beautiful blue eyes. I took the cat so he wouldn't have to go through that anymore. The poor cat had his hair knotted up so badly. It took me eight days to get the knots out of his hair. His name was **Kiki,** which was named after the girl who owned him. She abused him. I changed his name to Key co which is a guy's name in Spanish. In English, it means Frank.

Key co became better as time went on. Key co was being healed from being mistreated. It took a while for Key co to get the courage to come out during the day. Eventually he did. Then in time Key co got enough courage to go outside in the yard. Eventually, he loved it. Key-co became a whole different animal. My daughter's friend could not believe how different this cat had become in such a short time. This woman was a cat lover as well, she had cats of her own. She told me that I did a good job with the cat Key co. Key co loved to hear me sing to the Lord. Key co laid on my Bible on the kitchen table every morning. Poor Key co got a tumor. He had to be put to sleep. Key co was happy with me. He received the love he much needed before he died. Keyco was very old. It was getting hard for Keyco to jump up and down. Keyco had a good life before he died.

It has been quite an adventure taking care of animals through the years. One day while Noah, my grandson, and I were at the park, we saw two girls walking two dogs. One was little. One was big. The little one ran. Everyone was running after him. He was so cute. After that day, Noah cried. He wanted to go see the dog at the park. He would get my sandals and say, "Come on, Grandma, let's go see the puppy." I told him the puppy isn't there. When we saw the dogs, it was because the owners were taking them for a walk. There was no guarantee that we would see the dogs.

Every day we went through this routine. Then my daugther Noah's mom, said that we could go to the Humane Society and look for a dog. So Cassie Noah and I went to two different Humane Societies to look for a dog for Noah. I had just gotten my rent refund. So I told my daughter that I could pay for the dog, if we found one. Then we came across a dog that looked to be a good family dog. He was a mixture of labrador and collie, a good dog for a family. Good with kids. So we found our dog for the family.

He was all black and had long hair. I paid three hundred dollars for him. At first the dog was shy. He had come from another shelter in Oklahoma. His name was Lazy. He was very loving. In fact he was too loving. He licked all the time and everyone got mad and told him to stop. Of course, this dog didn't know what stop means. Sometimes I would say to Lazy, "What kind of language do you understand?" Then everyone would yell at him to stop. For a while Lazy didn't bother us when we had food. Then Lazy became comfortable with his surroundings and us. If we didn't watch our plate, our food would be gone. Every time when Noah's dad bought Noah a burrito, Lazy took it and ate it. Maybe Lazy had some Mexican in him as well. He began chewing up everything. The girls were mad that Lazy chewed up their underwear. Now this was getting very expensive. The things Lazy chewed up were costly. Everything was getting chewed up. My poor cats are being terrorized. Lazy had my black cat's whole head in his mouth. Poor BahBah. His name is Bopee or BahBah. We call him both.

Then my daughter and her friend were doing some yard work. They took part of the fence down. Now this was dangerous for Lazy. My daughter's friend hurt her neck. Now this is nerve racking. Without the fence being put back up, I was stressed and worried. My daugther didn't seem to care about my dogs safety. Every time Lazy goes out he almost gets hit by a car, motorcycle, or semi truck. Then my other daughter wanted to move in with her newborn, because she and her boyfriend were not getting along. She cannot stand Lazy. She yells at him constantly. So eventually my daughter and her friend took Lazy back to the Humane Society. The same one we got Lazy from. I cried and cried. My daughter said, "Oh mom, do you want to go back and get him?" I said no, Lazy deserves a better home. And a better family, a better life, than we could give him. If he stayed with us he would get killed by traffic. Besides he deserves a better life. At least he would be safe in the Humane Society. No matter how hard it is to give him up, I had to do what was best for the dog. Yes I'll cry and miss him. In time I will get over it. It takes time. Now he can be real happy and have a better life than I could give him. I hope that he has a good and happy life.

Next I get a dog that weighs five pounds. He is in need of a home. His ownner is sick with kidney dyallisis. So he cannot be with him all the time. So when the owner is gone the dog cries and howls. Because he does not like to be alone. And when the owner is home, he is too tired and sick to tend to the dog. The dogs name is chucky. He's a little applehead chiwawa dog. And he is cacausion all white. He is my new baby. I love him. I am such a animal lover. I am so blessed to have chucky. I think that chunky is blessed to have me and my family. Chucky won't have to be alone ever again. Their is some comfort for me as well to have chucky close to me. I am glad that the Lord brought us together. God is good all the time!

He's not late he is great! All the time. God has been watching over my children and me many times. Tammy was protected a lot as well. Tod has had his share of ongoing trials from the various homes he has previously lived in. Tod put himself through schooling and became an independent certified massage therapist. He also has an interest in Criminal Justice. He is trying to survive and succeed in this world. Then again that's what we all have been trying to do. Tammy has matured and had a child. Cassie still likes to learn. She stays active in the key club things, similar to Girl Scouts. She works in bookkeeping and accounting, and is going to school to further her education. Cassie bought a house. She is raising her son. God is good all the time. Cassie, my youngest daughter, is currently divorced. Her ex-husband is currently in the army reserves. They have a beautiful little boy named Noah. As for myself I am a widow. Sid and I got back together as husband and wife. We had marriage counseling from our pastor. We had our 12th anniversary. The next week Sid went to be with the Lord. It was as if he knew he was going to be with the Lord.

The night before Sid passed, we were at a bonfire with friends. Sid did not want to eat, talk or have a glass of water, nothing. Sid was fasting. He wasn't himself. We went to sleep and Sid never woke up. When Sid woke up he was in the arms of love, the Lord's. We had a beautiful memorial service for Sid. You could feel the Lord's presence. At the last minute I wrote a poem to Sid and read it. It was put on the program so people could read it. When I got to the church my friend Roberta said, "I thought you would like this." She handed me a beautiful flag that was purple with golden shimmers on it that my friend had made special for me. We knew I was supposed to dance at Sid's memorial. People said it was very much anointed. That the shimmers looked like the Glory of the Lord was falling upon me. They said it was beautiful. God made it very special. I danced to some music that Sid would always play. It is instrumental music and beautiful. This is the poem I wrote for Sid. On the program it said, 'A message from your wife."

I LOVED YOU AGAIN AND AGAIN

I loved you again and again.
You are a part of me, you are within.
Remembering the good times and the bad.
All the ups and downs we have had.
All the things that we have been through.
It's hard to go on without you… I am not sure what I should do.
I could hold my breath until I turn blue.
Or count my blessings for the time I had with you.
Surely you know what to do.
I will hang on to the memories we have had.
I will cherish them and be glad.
I look forward to being with you again and again.
There is a new beginning at hand.
I know you are in good hands.
You won't have to deal with any more demands.
You are where you have wanted to go for so long.
Now nothing can go wrong. You are where I want to be.
We will be together again, together for eternity.
I look forward to being with you again and again
when we do we will remember that we were best friends until we meet again.
Your loving wife.

We both worked at the healing rooms. I know I have been called to do this. I will live the rest of my days serving the Lord. I have written fifty-two short stories, children's books. It's a collection. The series is called Zoom it in. I pray whoever reads or listens to the books will be blessed.

Working in healing rooms ministries is in Saint Paul, Minnesota. There are other healing rooms in North Saint Paul and another healing rooms in the East side. In time the east side healing rooms closed. I've dedicated my life to using the gifts the Lord has given me to share and to bless other people.

In time I know the Lord will call me back to healing room's ministry. This is what I desire to do. I know the Lord put this desire within me. So I will be patient to wait on the Lord. We've come a long, long way. We may still have much further to go. In the meantime I'll keep doing what's right. Things will turn out right whether it is people or whether it is animals, I do what is placed in front of me. We are all of God's creation.

I will continue to do the Lords work. I will continue to pray for people in person or in requests. I will continue to be a prayer warrior. I will continue to be a workers of miracles. In the end when the Lord opens the door, I will walk through it. I will run into the right arms, the arms of love. For now I am in the arms of love, there's no other arms I'd rather be in, except the Lords. Now I have stopped running. Because I ran into the right arms, the arms of love.

HAPPY EVER AFTER

When you have been through disaster.
You don't feel like going out after. When
the winds shakes you to and fro. Remember
take a stand and let things go. Do not be out
of control. Let go and let God take the toll.
Soon you'll stroll down the street. Greeting

everybody you meet. Remember to be sweet.
Be discreet and be neat Do not pretend or bend
the end. In the end we will win. This is the
beginning and not the end. For lifes journey to
grow into maturity and for wisdom's delight to
be in sight. To have freedom to be right. To ask

for knowledge no you don't have to go to college.
For each and every day will be special in its own way.
There will never be two days the exact same.
This is not a game. This is a fact I know you by name.
You won't be put to shame so be happy ever after.

In time Tammy developed many health issues. She kept going to the doctor and hospital but they kept sending her home. I kept saying to Tammy that I didn't understand why they didn't keep her in the hospital to figure out what was wrong. I would take the baby when she was in the hospital or when she needed to rest. One day Tammy would be sick and weak and the next day she would be fine, energetic, enthusiastic and full of life. This went on for months. Me and my other daughter would tell her she still needed to rest but she said no. Tammy always wanted to go go go. She got me going back to church and involved in church activities. When she came out of the hospital after a four day stay, she came to my house with the baby and I took care of both of them. She seemed to get sicker though. She woke me up at 4:30 in the morning and told me that she was burning up. I gave her some Tylenol to bring the fever down. Finally the doctors discovered some things like she had a concussion from when she blacked out and fell down, she had bronchitis and vertigo and they found that she had syphilis. Syphilis is an infection in the blood. She first started blacking out a month before and she fell down and hurt herself. There was no one there to take care of the baby when she blacked out. The baby was 2 years old. Tammy passed out one day in front of the bathroom and she woke up to the baby slapping her on the face saying "Mama! Mama!" She couldn't take care of the baby and she would call me crying saying she hates her life because she couldn't do anything. She would call me gasping and out of breath and say that she is scared and she doesn't feel good and something is wrong. I sensed that she knew that she would be leaving the earth soon when she said she was scared. She called me back 5 minutes later saying she was going to call 911. I told her, what about the baby? She said she didn't know, so I told her to have the police bring the baby to me. Tammy said, "Ma! They cannot be making stops!" But I told her that the fire department, paramedics and police work together and that the police can bring the baby to me. So they took Tammy and the police brought the baby to me. Tammy was talking to the paramedics in the ambulance but then all of a sudden she stopped breathing. They worked on her for an hour trying to revive her. But it was too late, her heart gave out. I'm happy to know that she is with Jesus. But it hurts so bad. It is a horrible thing to go through for a parent to bury their child. It feel like somebody ripped my heart out of my chest and ripped it into a million pieces. It's so painful.

Some days I just sit and look at her pictures and I can't get dressed or going or anything. But I know she's in a better place. She is where we want to be. She is with Jesus now and living in peace. She was my sweet bonita.

MY SWEET BONITA

My sweet bonita, my joy, my pride
I couldn't wait to see you while you were growing inside
The first time I met you, I felt as thought I knew you
You shined like a trooper
You gave your time and love when someone needed you
I will cherish all the special things you have done
We will have a part of you forever
because of what Jesus has done
We will see you through your son
Don't worry, things will get done
One day we will meet again
In the end, I will always be your mama
And you will be my sweet bonita

www.ingramcontent.com/pod-product-compliance
Lightning Source LLC
LaVergne TN
LVHW091547060526
838200LV00036B/737